HIPPOLYTUS TEMPORIZES
& ION

OTHER BOOKS BY H.D.

H.D.

HIPPOLYTUS
TEMPORIZES
& ION

ADAPTATIONS OF TWO PLAYS
BY EURIPIDES

BY H.D.

INTRODUCTION BY CAROL CAMPER

A NEW DIRECTIONS BOOK

Frontispiece photograph of H.D., courtesy of the Schaffner Family Foundation.

Manufactured in the United States of America
New Directions Books are printed on acid-free paper.
Hippolytus Temporizes was first published by Black Swan Books in 1985. *Ion* was first
published by Black Swan Books in 1986. *Hippolytus Temporizes & Ion* first published as
New Directions Paperbook 967 in 2003.
Published simultaneously in Canada by Penguin Books Limited.

Library of Congress Cataloging-in-Publication Data

H. D. (Hilda Doolittle), 1886-1961.
  Hippolytus temporizes & Ion: adaptations of two plays by Euripides /
by H.D. ; introduction by Carol Camper.
    p. cm.
  ISBN 0-8112-1553-9 (pbk. : alk. paper)
  1. Hippolytus Temporizes (Greek mythology)—Drama. 2. Ion (Greek
mythology)—Drama. 3. Phaedra (Greek mythology)—Drama.   I. Title: Hippolytus
Temporizes & Ion. II. H. D. (Hilda Doolittle), 1886-1961. Hippolytus temporizes
III. Euripides. Ion.   IV. Euripides. Hippolytus. V. Camper, Carol. VI. Title.
  PS3507.O726I6 2003
  812'.52—dc22

                                    2003014394

New Directions Books are published for James Laughlin
by New Directions Publishing Corporation
80 Eighth Avenue, New York 10011

CONTENTS

INTRODUCTION
BY CAROL CAMPER

H.D.'s 1927 adaptation of Euripides' *Hippolytus Temporizes* and her 1937 translation of *Ion* appeared at midpoint in her career during a period marked by creative uncertainty and experimentation. Ever since her "Writing on the Wall" experience in Corfu in 1920 while traveling with her mother and Bryher (Winifred Ellerman, at that time H.D.'s lover), H.D. had struggled to place the hallucinatory experience within a psychological as well as creative context. She was not sure what to make of it, but she wanted to see it as an extension of the "gift" she had received from her Moravian mother, who had been a painter and musician. The elegant Imagist poems of her youth had established H.D.'s writing reputation, but now she was casting about for a medium that would better express her growing fascination with the unconscious and with esoteric traditions. From her earliest days as a poet, H.D. identified with Greek women poets and felt herself a kindred spirit. In deference to H.D.'s imaginative identification, Ezra Pound called her Dryad in 1918, but at that time neither could have foreseen where her fascination would take her, to the visionary epic poem, *Helen in Egypt (1954)*.

A modernist, H.D. valued clarity, economy, and contemporary idiom in her use of language. She also shared with other literary modernists a fascination with the unconscious and its expression in language and behavior. Related to this perception was her sense (shared with other women modernists such as Gertrude Stein, Marianne

Moore, Virginia Woolf, and Mina Loy) that women were writing both within and against a patriarchal literary tradition that had marginalized their work. For these modernists, the daunting task was to find, if not another language, then another way of using language to disrupt our culturally conditioned responses to art. Virginia Woolf's character Lily Briscoe in *To the Lighthouse* anguishes over a painting of the Ramsay summer home, stymied in her efforts to bring the shapes together in a new configuration. Thinking over her struggle, she imagines

> . . . tablets bearing sacred inscriptions, which if one could spell them out, would teach one everything, but they would never be offered openly, never made public. What art was there, known to love or cunning, by which one pressed through into those secret chambers?

These women modernists chose to stray from the correct, and thus conventional, deployment of language hoping themselves to spell out those inscriptions, so nearly decipherable and yet so out of reach.

When visiting Corfu in 1920, H.D. had visualized a kind of writing on the walls of her hotel room that calls to mind those tablets imagined by Lily Briscoe. As she relates the experience in *Tribute to Freud* (1956), a series of moving dots stretches out and very gradually forms three pictures: a tripod, a ladder, and an angel. These symbols H.D. identifies respectively as the tripod on which the priestess of Delphi sat, as Jacob's ladder, and as Nike or Victory. These images both terrified and elated H.D. She asked herself, "Am I looking at the Gorgon head, a suspect, an enemy to be dealt with? Or am I myself Perseus, the hero who is fighting for Truth and Wisdom?" Haunted by the experience, she entered psychoanalysis with Mary Chadwick in London and later with Hanns Sachs. But it was not until she entered a five-month analysis with Freud (March-June 1933, and resuming October-November 1934) that she had the breakthrough in self-understanding that allowed her to "place" the experience and also to resume her work as a poet. Her translation of *Ion* was completed during this period. A work of transition, it connects H.D.'s exploratory years to her re-emergence as poet.

During the period that preceded *Ion*, H D. worked on a cinema review, also acting in and helping edit films for Kenneth Macpherson; she wrote experimental novels, essays, and the *Hippolytus Temporizes* adaptation. Both *Hippolytus* and *Ion* are modern versions of classic plays. H.D. called *Ion* "a play after Euripides," and although it is a more faithful translation than her *Hippolytus* (which builds upon the original's dramatic structure of events but adds invented dialogue), *Ion*'s extensive commentary reflects not just H.D.'s understanding of Greek theater, but also her interpretation of Euripides' play. Of course, there is no translation without interpretation, the chief task of which, as George Steiner has observed, is to bring a heightened sense of the history of the text's language to the task so that the reader or audience finds in the syntax "a record of social being," a window on "the transforming energies of feeling" belonging to a culture (*After Babel*, p.26).

H.D. did not claim to be a scholar, and in *Bid Me to Live*, she expressed her dissatisfaction with the "grammarian" translators who treated the classics as "hoarded treasure" rather than try to make them "freshly minted." She had previously tried her hand at traditional translation with translations of choruses from *Hippolytus, Iphegenia in Aulis* (1919) and *The Bacchae* and *Hecuba* (1931). With each of these she maintained the metric repetitions of the originals.

Her work with *Hippolytus Temporizes*, however, unabashedly explores several favorite poetic themes from her own work that she believed she saw in Euripides as well: the struggle between intellect and emotion, between abstract detachment and passionate commitment, and the unhappy consequences of the Western dualistic habit of mind. Her Hippolytus is a monomaniacal purist devoted to Artemis because that goddess has loved his mother Hippolyta, who died giving birth to him nine months after her rape by Theseus. He seeks the shady solitude of the woods, flees people he regards with contempt, and worships the icy perfection of the chaste goddess with whom he desires to couple (his displaced desire for his mother). His stepmother Phaedra, consumed by her lust for Hippolytus, tricks him into thinking that her tent at the edge of the sea shelters Artemis and there seduces him. Both are doomed: Phaedra takes her own life, and Hippolytus is dashed upon the rocks. In H.D.'s version, both Phaedra and Hippolytus are absolutists in their one-sided view of life, but their single-mindedness also gives them their tragic grandeur. It is because Hippolytus has brought himself as close as humanly possible to the pristine life of his goddess that he is able to track her unerringly and surprise her in repose.

H.D.'s Hippolytus and Phaedra are more ambiguous than their counterparts in a standard translation like David Grene's in which Hippolytus speaks as a misogynist:

> Women! This coin which men find counterfeit!
> Why, why Lord Zeus, did you put them in the world,
> in the light of the sun? If you were so determined
> to breed the race of man, the source of it
> should not have been women. (p. 259)

However indifferent this Hippolytus may be toward women, he is deferential to the king and at home in the world, although he recognizes his world to be narrower than his father's:

> . . . I would wish to be
> first in the contests of the Greeks,
> but in the city I'd take second place
> and an enduring happy life among
> the best society who are my friends. (p. 274)

H.D.'s Hippolytus, in contrast, wants nothing to do with the city and its citizens. When his servant pleads with him to "come back," Hippolytus asks "Where?" as if to say, what once was home no longer exists. Phaedra responds with the identical question to her servant when asked to return to Theseus' palace. She, no less than Hippolytus, is estranged from the world she inhabits and spiteful in her dismissal of it:

> O how I hate,
> radiant, cold and drear,
> Greece with its headlands,
> Greece with its icy fervour,
> Greece with its high enchantment
> And endeavor,
> Greece and Greek cities
> for their arrogance. . . (p. 48)

Although H.D.'s Phaedra embraces sexuality and abandonment to passion, and although the gold, gold-red emblems of warmth with which H.D. surrounds her starkly contrast with the white, icy blue, and deep green symbols surrounding Hippolytus, H.D. is fascinated with the deeper, unexplored parallel between her two characters, a sameness which is at least as profound as their differences. So, while all translators can be said to re-create the original text ("finite mimesis," as George Steiner calls it), H.D. has additional ambitions. Through an act of sympathetic imagination based on her immersion in Greek culture, she wants to bring to the surface what she believes is latent in the text and to give it utterance. She wants to name what has not yet been named, not simply to restore or revive meaning of old texts, but in some cases, to bring into sharp focus what may have been blurred or even hidden.

Perhaps now it is easier to see why H.D. attached such great importance to her experience in Corfu and to see its connection with her Greek-themed work, including her translations. She knew that she was extraordinarily responsive to Greek art and literature; it gave her pure joy. She thought her insights went beyond the inventive to the truly profound, and she wanted to believe that her Corfu visions were a confirmation of that insight, not a delusion or a figment of an overstressed brain. Almost fifteen years after the experience, she placed it and her hopes before Freud and waited for his interpretation.

It is very clear from the H.D.-Bryher correspondence (published in the book *Analyzing Freud: Letters of H.D., Bryher and their Circle*) that Freud understood exactly what was at stake and that he approached his "response" very carefully. He began by sharing his collection of Greek antiquities with H.D., including his favorite piece, the Pallas Athene who was "perfect only she has lost her spear." His early sessions dealt with her household built around Bryher, Macpherson (then married to Bryher), and their shared daughter, Perdita. Freud and H.D. moved on to her childhood; the transference was effected (Freud resigned to representing "mother"), and they began to explore the multiple meanings surrounding the Corfu vision. As one might guess, Freud thought the vision was a troubling symptom; exploring her childhood with her, he evoked the female castration complex, but his interpretation did not end there. He affirmed that her symbols came from an "unexplored depth [in man's consciousness] [that] ran like a great stream or ocean underground, and the vast depth of that ocean was the same vast depth today as in Joseph's [or Jacob's] day" (*Tribute to Freud*, p. 71). Her picture-writing at Corfu (and by implication, her poet's vocabulary of images) was part of a universal language which spoke to all people across the centuries; it was not a delusion or wishful thinking to believe that her symbols caught up the traces of former civilizations, made connections with now forgotten ways of feeling, or could be a powerful force in exploring the harmful effects of some cultural beliefs (without ever using the terms, H.D. was a feminist and also a pacifist in her thinking).

Renewed and restored by her experience with Freud, H.D. took up a translation of *Ion*. Ion, the son of Apollo and the mortal Kreusa of Athens, is said to be the founder of Ionian culture and civilization. H.D. may have been initially attracted to *Ion* because Corfu (scene of the 1920 vision) is an Ionian island. However, her running commentary throughout the translation gives other reasons as well. She observes that Euripides was 60 at the time he wrote this play, an old man freed from military service but someone who, she thinks, "speaks through his boy-priest, Ion . . . of ecstasy before a miracle; the sun rises" (p. 15). She wants to counter the contemporary reading of ironies attached to the boy's praise of the Delphian oracular voice and to see in Euripides' play an affirmation of the mystical even among "that shifty, analytical, self-critical, experimental race of the city of Athens" (p. 14)—Euripides' contemporaries. H.D. repeatedly "sees into" the text to resurrect the spirit of the Greeks' beliefs, including the reverence with which they regarded the Delphic oracle.

In an extraordinary commentary passage, H.D. imagines what it was like at Delphi at the time of its eclipse by

Christianity. She sees frantic monks attempting to tear apart the temple with their hands, but: "So mighty was the inviolable spirit of this place that those monks, with their utmost fervour, could only dislodge a small number of its blocks, could only break off a small portion of the images of its façade and of its memorial figures, at turnings of the paved sacred way" (p. 19). An earthquake later sends down the walls "to crumble in frost and sun," but they reappear centuries later, reconstructed by archaeologists who have responded to the temple's beauty and power. Both this beauty and power are celebrated in *Ion* she believes, as reflected in her language.

Thus, during the performance of *Ion* in the age of Pericles, "Greek drama was religious in intention, directly allied to the temple ceremonies" (p. 9). Euripides stages his play in front of and within the temple at Delphi to explore the drama of a woman who believes herself to be betrayed by both man (her husband) and by the god who had impregnated her. Kreousa attempts to poison Ion when she fails to recognize him as her son by Apollo and sees instead an outsider and usurper of her throne. When the attempted poisoning is thwarted, she faces death by stoning, and her principle antagonist and pursuer is none other than her son. Ion finds Kreousa cowering by the altar to Phoebus Apollo where she has taken refuge and, in a surprising shift, rather than evoke the ancient law of religious sanctuary, she instead feels herself protected by the very god she had previously felt abandoned and betrayed by. She says (in H.D.'s translation): "I am safe with the god;/my body is his, by right." And Ion drifts away from the overblown denunciation with which he initially confronted Kreousa ("O face of a monster, what dragon begot you?") and almost pleads, "I was always his [Apollo's] near-son" (p. 94)—as if to acknowledge the legitimacy of Kreousa's claims, however unconsciously.

By the end of the play, all is revealed, the mystery of Ion's birth and abandonment made clear, and everyone returns to their customary expressions of piety. But at the heart of the play is Kreousa' s crisis of belief and the unknowable mystery of the gods' ways. H.D.'s approach stresses the characters' unconscious gropings toward the truth of their situation. To H.D.'s way of thinking, the unconscious can lead to disintegration and tragedy but it can also lead to their opposite, as it does in this play. When H.D. offers the following translation of Pallas Athene's final speech in *Ion,* she emphasizes its double reading:

> "the gods' pace moves slow,
> do they forget?
> no;
> blessed be the man
> who waits
> (nor doubts)
> for the end
> of the intricate
> plan. (p. 118)

Athena appeals to humans' piety to silence their doubts about the gods' wisdom and justice; H.D. would also have us see in the statement the need to be patient with the tortuous ways of the unconscious. As she says in her commentary to this play, Athene "pleas for the great force of the under-mind or the unconscious that so often, on the point of blazing upward into the glory of inspirational thought, flares, by a sudden law of compensation, down, making for tragedy, disharmony, disruption, disintegrations, but in the end, O, in the end, if we have patience to wait, she says, if we have penetration and faith and the desire to actually follow all those hidden subterranean forces, how great is our reward" (p. 112).

In Euripides' *Ion* the Pythian priestess, who had discovered Ion the abandoned infant and brought him up as temple keeper, makes possible the formal recognition of mother and son, just as she is the mediator between the world of men and the universe of the gods. This is the role H.D. had imagined for herself at Corfu when she saw the image of the tripod, although she would not interpret the ways of the gods to man but rather the mysterious ways of our other selves, our unconscious selves as we can read them through language.

Freud wrote to H.D. in February 1937 after receiving a copy of the *Ion* translation. He wrote, "Deeply moved by the play (which I had not known before) and no less by your comments, especially those referring to the end, where you extol the victory of reason over passions, I send you the expression of my admiration and kindest regards" (*Tribute to Freud*, p. 194). It was the last translation or adaptation H.D. was to do. She moved on to *Helen in Egypt*, a sweeping epic of healing and integration centered on the figure of Helen who seeks to transcend the crippling dualism, especially the one binding eros and thanatos, a topic dear to her guide/mentor/admirer Freud as well.

—Carol Camper

HIPPOLYTUS
TEMPORIZES
& ION

HIPPOLYTUS
TEMPORIZES

I worship the greatest first—
(it were sweet the couch,
the brighter ripple of cloth
over the dipped fleece;
the thought: her bones
under the flesh are white
as sand which along a beach
covers but keeps the print
of the crescent shapes beneath:
I thought:
between cloth and fleece,
so her body lies.)

I worship first the great—
(ah, sweet, your eyes—
what God, invoked in Crete,
gave them the gift to part
as the Sidonian myrtle-flower
suddenly, wide and swart,
then swiftly,
the eye-lids having provoked our hearts—
as suddenly beat and close.)

I worship the feet, flawless,
that haunt the hills—
(ah, sweet, dare I think,
beneath fetter of golden clasp,
of the rhythm, the fall and rise
of yours, carven, slight
beneath straps of gold that keep
their slender beauty caught,
like wings and bodies
of trapped birds.)

I worship the greatest first—
(suddenly into my brain—
the flash of sun on the snow,
the fringe of light and the drift,
the crest and the hill-shadow—
ah, surely now I forget,
ah, splendour, my goddess turns;
or was it the sudden heat,
beneath quivering of molten flesh,
of veins, purple as violets?)

ISLES OF GREECE
Spring, 1920

PEOPLE OF THE PLAY

Hippolytus: son of Theseus and Hippolyta
Hyperides: courtier of Athens
Leader of the Huntsmen
Band of Huntsmen
Boy: from a wrecked Cyprian vessel

Phædra: wife of Theseus, King of Athens
Myrrhina: serving-lady to Phædra
Nurse: to Phædra
Band of serving-women
Servants, musicians, etc.

Artemis
Helios

‑ⅼⅼⅼ‑

THE ARGUMENT

THIS *is the familiar story of Theseus of Athens. Hippolytus, his son and the child of Hippolyta, inflames a later wife, the Cretan princess, Phædra, in her palace outside Trœzen in Attica. Theseus, King of Athens, finds his rival in his own son, the step-son of his foreign queen.*

How Hippolytus returns the affection so secretly and tragically bestowed has become a legend, the prototype of unrequited passion for many centuries. Hippolytus is his mother again, frozen lover of the forest which maintains personal form for him in the ever-present vision, yea, even the bodily presence of the goddess Artemis.

Phædra by a trick (as we see in the second act of this play) gains the passion of the youth. The boy, as tradition has always maintained, in a frenzied drive along an infuriated seacoast, is broken and mercilessly battered by the waves. The consequence of his death to two of the Olympians is here set forth in the final act of this tragedy, HIPPOLYTUS TEMPORIZES.

*Below Trœzen. A wild gorge or ravine cuts through the trees on to a flat,
sandy beach.*

Artemis   I HEARD the intolerable rhythm
and sound of prayer,
so I have hidden
where no mortals are,
no sycophant of priest
to mar my ease,
climbing impassible stairs
of rock
and forest shale
and barriers of trees:

someone will come
after I shun this place
and set a circle,
blunt end up,
of stones,
flattened and hewn,
and pile an altar,
but I shall have gone further
toward loftier barrier,
mightier trees;
bear, wolf and pard
I will entice with me,
that eyes' black fire
or yellow
flatter,
conjure,
feed desire,
conspire,
lead me yet further

to some loftier shelf,
untrodden;

unappeased,
I will disport at ease
and wait;
I will engage in thought and plot with
    earth
how we may best efface
from Elæa
and all stony Peloponnese,
from wild Arcadia
and the Isthmian straits,
from Thrace and Locrian hills,
(as isles are sunk
in overwhelming seas),
all Grecian cities
with the wild arbutus
and the luminous trees.

Enter HIPPOLYTUS, *stumbling forward, uncertain in the half-light.*

Hippolytus   Here in the night,
here in the salt-whipped air,
you hide;
but where,
where,
where,
O mistress of the tide-line of the sea,
of the deep-sea self
and the implacable tide?

Artemis   Again,
again,
intolerable prayer.

Hippolytus   I found trace of you on the mountain
    stair,
within a fern-lined crevice,
for the snare
set for a wild bird

showed who had been there,
the trap was sprung and the wild bird
    was free;
queen of the peaked hills,
I have followed three
ecstatic linnets
who bewitched must bear
bright wings aloft
to turn and whirr and fall,
having no motive but to whirr and
    whirr,
to circle and to chatter and to care
for nothing further
than to scream and call,
so I have learned their bird-notes
and so follow
like a wild linnet,
Artemis,
Artemis—

Artemis   O madness of wood-speech—

Hippolytus   I have implored the adder
and the bear,
the lynx,
the pard,
the panther
for some prayer,
some charm,
some peril to entrap your feet;
I have intrigued for many days
to meet
some kindly serpent
who might name your name,
so I might lay in wait
to lure, to hiss
like a wood-creature,
Artemis,
Artemis—

Artemis	He would betray—
Hippolytus	Wild, wild, wild, wild, O fair, I have cajoled, implored, seared the bright air with your bright name that like an arrow tears my heart to speak it; I have imperilled, shamed the very stars with brighter shaft, with more imperious flame of blinding light and fervour, Artemis—
Artemis	Again.
Hippolytus	Artemis, Artemis, Artemis, are you near? O listen, pause and hear, bright queen and phantom—
Artemis	He bends and touches the inviolate sand—
Hippolytus	O wild, wild, wild, O sweet,

is this the shape and pattern
of your feet
or some bright flower
blown here from other lands?
is this some blossom,
wafted from your hands,
or the white trail of phosphorescent
    sea?
is this flower shaken from some woodland
    tree
or have the stars trailed down
to brush the land?

Artemis   The broken weed,
the scattered broken shell—

Hippolytus   Wild,
wild,
wild,
wild,
O dear,
I have inflamed and torn the dispassionate
    air
with sound of flute
and note of song
and metre—

Artemis   I fear—

Hippolytus   There,
there,
there,
there I see—

Artemis   Ah me—

Hippolytus   There,
there,

there,
there,
O star,
queen of the sea-cliff
and the mountainous air
that stings and burns
and lightens us like wine,
O queen and mistress—

Artemis   Beware—

Hippolytus   Wondrous,
O fair,
like some tall supple sapling
or some rare
young warrior
with his glittering arms and spear,
call, call
your silver wolf-hounds,
dart your spear,
and fling your arrows,
can they rend and tear
and wound me
as the arrows of your hair
that flame and burn
as if some travelling meteor
had dropped its mantle
where the laurels burn?
do I—I fear?
nay goddess, exquisite and dear—
O turn—

Artemis   I must be off,
Hippolytus, you have crossed
my path
too often—

Hippolytus   Witness each copse and glen,

where every time I found you,
I set up
a lesser goddess,
silver-cold
and wrought
by the most exquisite craftsmen—

Artemis   No craftsman may imprison
my swift feet—

Hippolytus Nay, wild and sweet,
but song may yet entrap you,
fire and rhythm
may yet contain the ecstasy
and the heat
cold like white lightning—

Artemis   O what,
what,
what, Hippolytus,
do you seek?

Hippolytus I seek as a wood-lover,
O wild heart,
the very pulse and passion of your feet,
I scale the height for wild deer
but I ask
of every stone upturned,
of the moss print,
of scattered shells
and broken acorn cups,
of every grass blade trodden
and the earth
sprinkled with unaccustomed silver
     drift
of sand
and delicate seed-pearls
from the east,

Artemis,
Artemis,
Artemis,
has she passed?

Artemis   You waste your life
              in shadowing Artemis.

Hippolytus Can any waste his life
              in fervid worship?

Artemis   What of the city,
              the demands of kingship?

Hippolytus My city is the forest,
              I, its high priest—

Artemis   There is a goddess
              and a priest who frowns—

Hippolytus You have no rival
              in the windless towns—

Artemis   The streets are fervid,
              the town squares are rife—

Hippolytus With what, O mistress,
              that concerns our life?

Artemis   The streets are rabid
              with small talk and dire—

Hippolytus What talk, O queen,
              intolerate, white like fire?

Artemis   I stand intolerate with disgust,
              not hate—

Hippolytus	What tale has reached you, of what wicked thing?
Artemis	A tale of Athens' queen, of Athens' king—
Hippolytus	Alas, my dotard sire, my captured father—
Artemis	Beware the capturer who may snare another—
Hippolytus	You speak, O queen, an impotent phrase and shame me who but praise your beauty O white flower, O passionate maid—
Artemis	How do I mock? speak, should I share detachment, chastity and fervid thought with *her?*
Hippolytus	What pointless question— tell me if you dare what day has passed and witnessed my neglect, what altar has been empty or what fair white statue of what distant fane accosts you, to complain that its bright throat was bare of any wild flower?

Artemis	Alas,
	no day
	has witnessed lack of prayer,
	alas, no statue
	ever has been bare
	of mountain lily
	or wild-lily chaplet;
	alas,
	the very forests
	bend and sway,
	bearing aloft frail incense
	from the fires
	that you have lit
	on every altar base;
	alas, no place is empty of you
	and your perilous fervour—
Hippolytus	Then stay,
	stay,
	stay—
Artemis	Alas,
	alas,
	alas,
	I would escape,
	myself escape from all men's songs
	and praying;
	I can not breathe,
	I can not rest nor sleep;
	ever and ever as the wild trees, soft,
	bend over to embrace
	and breathe me back,
	back to the very substance of the forest,
	at just that moment
	as I loose my shape,
	become immortal, evanescent,
	essence of wood-things
	and no more a goddess,
	at just that moment

when I would attain immortal sustenance
and gain my rest,
some prayer arises dimming tree and
    forest
and I must answer those who pray the
    goddess,
a goddess rise and help
or slay
or heal or bless;
I must retain the god-like attribute
when such as you appeal;
ah, you, you most,
you trap, you trick, you take—
I traced this runnel
from the farthest hills
to this sea-shelter,
this remote sea-cove,
lonely, immanent, where peril
I thought had made all safe,
but you,
you like a bird,
Hippolytus,
must follow—

Hippolytus   O fair—

Artemis   Have I no peace,
no quiet anywhere?
you trick,
you trap, Hippolytus,
a goddess in your snare.

Hippolytus   Say rather
you have trapped,
have stricken me—

Artemis   I have not lured you here
nor anywhere—

Hippolytus	There is a lure more potent than mere prayer—
Artemis	What lure, what lure, Hippolytus— but beware—
Hippolytus	The lure of frenzied feet, of webbed gold hair—
Artemis	I am not woman nor of womankind—
Hippolytus	To such, O mistress, I am blind, blind, blind—
Artemis	What of this rumour that provokes the streets—
Hippolytus	Rumour of bees, of wasps, of unclean tame beasts—
Artemis	Rumour of bees and wasps and of dishonour—
Hippolytus	O queen, O mistress, speak not of that fever—
Artemis	Yea, I am told charms call you to her favour—
Hippolytus	Not I—not I—I am no wanton's lover—
Artemis	This wanton holds a place besides a king—
Hippolytus	A king of cities, of no spirit-bride—

Artemis	But go—but go— they say her lust invokes—
Hippolytus	Nothing, I say nothing my fire provokes—
Artemis	I do not stay to rival anyone—
Voices *(distant)*	*Never in porch or corridor* *can love come,* *never to us who died young,* *long ago,* *long ago.*
Hippolytus	What are these voices?
Artemis	These are my maidens who are wroth to see me loitering with a mortal.
Hippolytus	I am no mortal.
Artemis	Boastful and hot as ever.
Hippolytus	Hot on the trail, hot, hot, in my desire to trace you in the forest, in the brake, in tangle of the wild larch, through the stretch of pine and poplar where the intoxicant scent reels and transports me of the flowering wild grapes—

Artemis	The grapes give stronger wine in Trœzen town—
Hippolytus	No wine can tempt me from the blossoming wood—
Artemis	Red roses burn away the flowering tree—
Hippolytus	Nay, let me share your solitude by the sea—
Artemis	Share, share the mind with fierce companion mind, poetic frenzy with another blind with rapturous fire of the enchanter's harp, share, share the mind or love with any lover, but beware: the rapture of my loneliest crags none share—
Hippolytus	But I— but I— following the staggering wild deer and fleet hind, breaking the wood-branch, struggling with the vine that falls and swings and tangles as it sways, I follow and I share abandonment with Artemis.
Artemis	None share but womankind.

Voices *(distant)*	*Never in porch or corridor* *can love come,* *never to us who died young,* *long ago,* *long ago.*
Hippolytus	What curious echo.
Artemis	My maidens; go, go, go—
Hippolytus	Where can I go for you are everywhere—
Artemis	Not where the Cyprian weaves her perilous snare.
Hippolytus	You lie— *this* is no place to speak her name—
Artemis	Her name is everywhere, her ways are dire—
Hippolytus	Do you, white goddess, slander spirit-fire?
Artemis	Spirit of lust you mean, the dangerous mother—
Hippolytus	Mistress of danger, aye, and luminous æther—
Artemis	You mean the cruel one, the Cytherian?
Hippolytus	You, you are cruel; no, I mean another—

Artemis	What spirit, speak, and who is this I slander?
Hippolytus	You do belittle a most gracious name—
Artemis	What name, what spirit, devot of what fane?
Hippolytus	Her fane the forest is, and I her lover—
Artemis	I say our paths part and our ways forever—
Hippolytus	Nay, nay, we meet in deep love for another—
Artemis	What love, what love may bind our hearts together?
Hippolytus	Love of Hippolyta, my loveliest mother.
Artemis	You had the hills, the willows, white ash, poplar blent into one form, true, lithe tree-boughs for a mother.
Hippolytus	Hippolyta, the very name a rill, a river or a faun, and evil for a father.
Artemis	Theseus is great.

Hippolytus	You speak, O queen, impotent phrase and mock the sting, the pain, you, you alone of all the gods who take unfailing worship from me.
Artemis	No mortal measures stature with a spirit.
Hippolytus	But spirits grieve and grow like mortals, desperate.
Artemis	My spirit, rapturous, scales Olympos' height.
Hippolytus	Not thine, not thine, not thine, O Artemis, it haunts the wood-path, desolate even as mine.
Artemis	You desecrate.
Hippolytus	You shun Olympos, Artemis, and its shale holds nothing for you sweeter than the forest, no ecstasy holier than the vine's cold scent, the fragrance of the larch and the wild pine, no tenderness can keep you

in God's palace
from whelps that wander
desolate at night.

Artemis　　　You are no whelp
of mine.

Hippolytus　　As she was yours,
so I—I am your own—

Artemis　　　No; Athens claims you
and the Athenian throne—

Hippolytus　　I would not rule,
O I would only rest,
forgetting everything
in this cold place.

Artemis　　　You are half mortal,
and a mortal's heart
is never wholly god-like,
still and cold.

Hippolytus　　No, no,
I am not mortal;
only think
how my great mother
shaped me to her will;
I was her heart within her
and her steel;
O she was proud and valiant,
swift to kill,
relentless and impartial,
warrior still,
giving no space to woman vagaries
and all the woman weakness and wan
　　ill,
valiant and resolute and untamed

until
she bore me
for a lance,
a sword,
a spear.

Artemis   Rashly;
                   too late repented and so died—

Hippolytus   O say it not,
                   impartial, hard with pride;
                   you could have saved her
                   had you had the heart,
                   one grain, one seed of human kindly
                       love,
                   how is it you
                   who seek in wind and wet
                   the ferret as she writhes,
                   the smallest fox,
                   the deer in pain,
                   could not have saved
                   Hippolyta
                   with arrow-swift
                   white lightning
                   for her beauty?

Artemis   Gods may not
                   cut athwart
                   a mortal's fate.

Hippolytus   Then are the gods
                   no greater than mere men?

Artemis   Sometimes less great.

Hippolytus   You mock,
                   cryptic and cold,
                   hard and imperious,

you might have saved
(who save the tiniest fox),
my mother.

Artemis

I will not stay and argue with a man,
for you are that,
for all your fragile and imperious
    length,
your pale set features
and your woman's grace.

Hippolytus

A woman's grace?
I who have conquered
all this perilous cliff
and climbed the shale—

Artemis

And she,
did our alert Hippolyta less?

Hippolytus

O mock me not,
mock not
my bitterness;
I know, I kneel,
her white soul is my strength,
let me stay with you as she stayed,
let me hunt with you,
rest by your white side,
take me,
a servant.

Artemis

Hippolyta had rare grace
and holiness;
she was a woman.

Hippolytus

But I, but I,
her white soul lives in me,
Hippolyta lives in me,
in my taut brain,

in all these thoughts
you say temper my prayers,
Hippolyta is my arrow-point,
my spear,
she listens now
in every bright and evanescent leaf,
she hears.

Artemis   Hippolyta,
my friend,
chaste queen and ally,
valiant and fervid amazon
is dead.

Hippolytus   O if she were,
how simple,
O how meet,
for I would walk in Athens like a man,
or like a prince,
I'd stroll through Trœzen's street,
not like a mad man
or a simple youth,
struck down with some implacable
    malady
of dream or frenzy
or mere impotence,
O if Hippolyta were only dead in me,
then I would sit in front of all the
    throng,
as Theseus bids me in the banquet
    hall,
smiling and suave,
all of the courtier,
great Theseus as you call him,
bids me be;
O if Hippolyta were dead in me.

Artemis   You weep—

Hippolytus	Yea, all the woman's wit and woman's grace you taunt me with, lives though my mother died; and you it was, who tend the merest mole, let her slip from me, even as I lay, a weakling and an infant in her arms, gone marble; not my weight, nor all my just-born heat could comfort her, and you, you, you, goddess, the first, the great, let her so perish, who protect the gull, the swallow, the wild owl, the tern.
Artemis	Peace, child.
Hippolytus	Yes, let me rest, you are the mother, you the nearest; you are a spirit, spirit even as she, somewhere not here; you, you are somewhere else, not here, I know; I am not here while thus I talk with you.

Artemis	Seek not too far—
Hippolytus	Or seek, seek, seek only a little further.
Artemis	Tempt not the gods—
Hippolytus	Are gods then weak like mortals? can we tempt?
Artemis	Too well.
Hippolytus	Mother.
Artemis	Nay, nay, you are no son, no child of mine, in you yet lives the strong and valiant soul of Theseus of Athens; should I cherish here, this prince of Athens, bid him to betray his kingship and the kings that after him may sway all Attica, then were the gods, Zeus, Pallas and Another wroth with me.

She bends back her head, seeming to search the air above her.

> Do you not sense nor see
> this fluttering
> of bright garments
> and bright wings?

the woods are mine
but not the hearts of kings.

*Halloing from a distance. The whole of the forest becomes blurred in a
curious white mist. As the mist gradually disperses,* HIPPOLYTUS *is
seen wandering as if struck blind or with fear of blindness.*

HYPERIDES *enters, wandering across the sand, not perceiving the prince.*

Hyperides   Religion is all very well I say,
yea,
let religion have its place,
and prayer
in temple and in temple corridor,
lay the white-grape
in the sun-smitten porch,
the knot of fish upon Poseidon's floor,
the wild-grape
on the threshold of the king
of frenzy
to Iacchos—it is well;
let tall Athene have the broken spear,
give Helios the harp
and the harp string;
yea, worship is a thing
that's well enough
in its own place,
in porch and corridor;
what I object to
is this wilfulness
that frets
that rages
that inhibits mirth,
this boy infatuation
for a wraith;
a wraith?
what sound?
only the merest thrush

or summer owl;
yea, even this wild-wood worship
has its place,

(Louder) Yea, I have said
even the wilderness
should have its share,
an altar here,
a heap of round stones there;

(He shouts) Yea,
I have said
even the wilderness
should have its share
of praise.

He shudders suddenly and starts as he half discerns the wraith-form of
HIPPOLYTUS.

Queen,
goddess,
sorceress,

HIPPOLYTUS *appears as in a maze. He gropes forward.*

Hyperides Gods,
I am growing murky
with white sweat,
what trick,
what game,
why do you torture us?

Hippolytus Who are you?

Hyperides O prince have done
with all this murky game,
come out,
come forth,
demand your place in life,

                    your share in power
and social intercourse;
what is it?
why this taut
and stiffened frame,
these eyes
fixed like the wild cat?
you are the victim of some evil charm
or devil magic.

Hippolytus   No, no, Hyperides,
I see you well,
I know you,
you are just like all the rest;
your eyes are round and full
yet dark with fright,
your limbs are firm and carved of some
      dark bronze,
your head is set
like some young Pythian god;
you are a statue in the halls of kings—
but leave me.

Hyperides   Part of my duty,
part of my content,
my fate, indeed my greatest happiness
is to be servant of a mighty prince,
son of great Theseus,
Athens' potentate.

Hippolytus   Your Theseus,
your Athens
make me sick.

Hyperides   It charms you to be wilful.

Hippolytus   I hate you
and your courtier-like suave face.

Hyperides	Are you (I ask in all solicitude), so much then, the superior of us all?
Hippolytus	Ask of the wrestling field, the track of Limnas.
Hyperides	Your steeds are swifter, your white arm most fit, but of your mind?
Hippolytus	My mind is well enough in solitude.
Hyperides	Prince, I too would enjoy to hunt still further in the forest, but the king, Theseus commands—
Hippolytus	Tell to your king, your Theseus, that his son seeks in the hills, the valleys, in the plains, the rivers, to recall the trace of one long since forgotten.
Hyperides	Far better for your own inheritance as son and prince, than that late Amazon—
Hippolytus	Ah speak—speak on— how gladly will this place

be joyous witness
of blood-sacrifice.

Hyperides   Prince,
peace,
I do assure you I but sought,
when all the other courtiers took fright,
the wild-wood for you;
and I followed straight
the upright vertical steep cliff
then down again vertical
even though I fell.

Hippolytus   I tell you
you are fit to stand
within the halls of kings
in bronze,
the perfect servant
of the imperfect prince.

Hyperides   Then come.

Hippolytus   Why do you urge me;
I am well enough.

Hyperides   Come back.

Hippolytus   Where?

Hyperides   Home.

Hippolytus   That palace with its incense
and its love-rites?

Hyperides   Surely the palace
is a gracious place,
and the set palace garden with its terrace,
its fountains,

                    its impenetrable grove
                    of sweet myrtle,
                    its beds of hidden violets.

Hippolytus   That woman
                    with her various tricks
                    and magic?

Hyperides   The queen?

Hippolytus   Queen of your sort,
                    queen of the weakling
                    king,
                    Theseus of Athens.

Hyperides   My lord—

Hippolytus   Yes, tell the king
                    his son has jeered at him,
                    shout to the woods
                    that he has gained no love
                    with all his senile Greek urbanities;
                    tell Theseus of Athens he begot
                    when once in all his life
                    he showed his strength
                    (and that ignobly),
                    a spear, a shaft, of lightning
                    for a son,
                    and that son loves in all the world
                    no queen
                    of spice and perfume
                    but the immortal flower
                    bred in the storm,
                    sister of ice and wind,
                    queen only of the soul,
                    white Artemis.

The members of the band of hunters have entered gradually and grouped themselves about the two.

Hyperides	He rages still.
Huntsman	Let him rage on, the fiercer, soonest over.
Hippolytus	Rage, rage, rage, rage, O wonder of wild, wild feet, O glistening of bright hair—

The boy from a wrecked Cyprian vessel steps forward.

Boy	But where?
Hippolytus	O here, O there, O here and there and nowhere— now she is here, and now she has dismayed my very eye-balls, played some trick upon me, burning with vivid brilliance but to mock with greater darkness and so disappear.
Boy	The sun climbs o'er the hill.
Hippolytus	Then is it day?
Hyperides	Alas, you do display a curious humour—

Hippolytus	Hyperides,
	whose name might fire
	and blaze and gleam
	a trail like moon-stones
	upon quiet water—
	but a fool—
Hyperides	My lord—
Hippolytus	Go, go, go, go,
	you tool of indolent Theseus,
	with your friendly hirelings,
	sycophant,
	panderer,
	go, for you are not worthy even to
	kneel
	on this white sand
	nor feel anything
	of the wonder of this land—
Hyperides	My prince, we find the sunrise
	beautiful—
Hippolytus	Poor ignorant knave—
Boy	What, prince, has driven you wild?
Hippolytus	Who are you, child?
Boy	I am a stranger from a broken keel,
	our boat foundered—
Hippolytus	But you kneel—
Boy	To you,
	who have such passion in your eyes,
	I am reminded of the drowning men—

Hippolytus	I drown in forest waves of green and foam—
Hyperides	Come then, come home—
Hippolytus	Hyperides, Hyperides, be off—
Hyperides	O prince, be reasonable—
Hippolytus	O obstinate fool— what is your reason to this wild unrest?
Hyperides	Would you have music then?
Hippolytus	Music?
Hyperides	I sent back for the band of singing men when we first found you—
Hippolytus	Music?
Hyperides *(to the* *musicians)*	Begin.

The musicians form in usual, conventional dance form. They chant or
sing as if before some imaginary altar.

Hippolytus	O tear the strings, have done with mockery of set and stated time

of word and metre;
have done with all that tune,
throw the lyre down;
what word, what word
can tell the sudden rhythm
of her white feet
that even as a bird wing
fled?

Hyperides   Patience, O prince,
the form is well enough,
we patterned that
on the iambics brought
but late,
by way of Cos
to Attica.

Hippolytus   What island impudence;
O well enough
to frame a slight song
that some singing lad
proclaims within the hall
of some Demeter
stately and still,
or in a festival,
beats out to modulate the dancing feet
of country choristers.

Hyperides   What is song then,
but measure to beat out
the tune
for feet to move by?

Hippolytus   Feet, feet, feet, feet,
what of the head, the heart,
the frenzy that swims up
like sudden tide

of full storm-sea
at sun-down?

Hyperides   You cannot catch the sea
within a song.

Hippolytus   What is song for,
what use is song at all,
if it cannot imprison all the sea,
if it cannot beat down
in avalanche of fervour even the wind,
if it cannot drown out
our human terror?

Hyperides   Song is a thing,
fitted to time and measure.

Hippolytus   Like our Hyperides'
subtle mind's
bright treasure—

Hyperides   O prince,
this peevish fit
is juvenile,
song has been set
by your great ancestors,
by singing muses,
by the priest that sings
before your father's palace even now,
in his own temple
up in Trœzen yonder,
come back prince,
to the temple and the altar.

Hippolytus   Can you not see or feel?

Hyperides   My prince, we feel
the beauty of this sunrise—

Hippolytus	You feel nothing at all, and are a blatant hypocrite who think to humour a mad prince—
Hyperides	We see the—ah— splendour—yea— of wood and tree—
Hippolytus	Be off, be gone, your very presence is an insult to this stately wood-land and the holy shore, you pandering nobleman, you courtly bore and sycophant.
Hyperides	Worse, worse and more—
Hippolytus	More and much worse will come if you delay, O go, begone tiresome young idiot—
Hyperides	And fool—
Hippolytus	Fool if you will, and gaping flattering tool of impotent Theseus—
Hyperides	Impotent?
Hippolytus	If he were powerful and real in his pretended fervour, then Phædra—
Hyperides	Hist— take care—

Hippolytus	Take care of nothing, not of gaping layers of men, if they are men at all, who neither see, nor think, nor hear nor feel—
Hyperides	Come, come—
Hippolytus	You'd best be gone— say to the king that prince Hippolytus is safe, for I—I know you follow me to spy.
Hyperides	Nay king—
Hippolytus	Yes, all of you begone, I would remain alone—
Hyperides	Prince, I must stay—
Hippolytus	Not you, not you, you are the worst of all, if you must have a reason, then go say that prince Hippolytus sent you back to fetch the statue by the hedge of flowering bay, the garden statue for this lonely sand—
Hyperides	Will the king understand?
Hippolytus	Have I not always given command to place statues by running waters

	and in each rare place I hunted?
Hyperides	Yes, this is true.
Hippolytus	Go, go then all of you, make a procession, bringing flowers and say, "Hippolytus waits, Hippolytus waits alone until we come."
Hyperides *(to the* *musicians)*	Prepare the way, make festival and rite of this, we go.

Exit HYPERIDES, *huntsmen and musicians.*

Hippolytus	I am alone—
Boy	O queen, who saved us gracious from the sea, we pray—
Hippolytus	Do you delay?
Boy	I could not go and leave you here, so wild, with eyes so lit with frenzy and so prone to sudden feverish trembling; do you see then, this lady in the bush and tree?

Hippolytus	I do not see my queen; O I am tired and weary in the day, the night was long but reft with light and spray like blossoming foam.
Boy	Will you not lie along this pelt and rest?

The BOY *unfastens his cloak and lays it upon the sand.*

> The breath of fields is in it
> and of loam.

HIPPOLYTUS *flings himself face downward on the cloak.*

Hippolytus	I hear her voice, I clasp her luminous knees—
Boy	It seems his lady is like mine at home—
Hippolytus	I breathe the fragrance of her hands like wine—
Boy	Yes, she is much, is very much like mine—
Hippolytus	I pray, I pray, I pray that you but come—
Boy	She will come for they always do with prayer—
Hippolytus	I feel her breath, intoxicant, clear air—

Boy	They say her breath is the white violet flower—
Hippolytus	You, you are right, white violets for her hair—
Boy	Her knees are lustrous, her white forehead shines—
Hippolytus	Shines in the mist, bound with its luminous band—
Boy	Her crown is plaited myrtle and rose-stem—
Hippolytus	I do not hear your words, your voice is song—
Boy	Sleep drowns him now, poor prince, see he is gone—
Hippolytus	Not gone—not gone— watch for me, lest she come—
Boy	Prince, I will wait, they go to fetch her now—
Hippolytus	Her statue—but herself— make prayer for me—
Boy	I will entreat the wild-wood and the sea—
Hippolytus	Sing, sing, sing, sing, your song may bring her here—

Boy I sing, I watch, I wait
with fervid prayer.

The BOY *stoops over* HIPPOLYTUS *to fold the cloak about him.*

He sleeps.

Voices *Never in porch or corridor*
(far distant) *did love come,*
never to us who died young
long ago,
long ago.

ACT II

Evening (the same strip of seacoast. The statue of ARTEMIS *has been set up).*

Phædra

O HOW I HATE,
radiant, cold and drear,
Greece with its headlands,
Greece with icy fervour,
Greece with its high enchantment
and endeavour,
Greece and Greek cities
for their arrogance,
each with particular grace,
each claiming god
for some peculiar ardour,
differing each from each,
yet each complete,
spirit, mind, arrogance
of small material wealth,
each soul unto itself;
is there no merging,
no hint of the east?
no carelessness
nor impetuousness of speech?
can no one greet
my south!
O glorious,
sweet,
red, wild pomegranate-mouth?
O my heart breaks and burns,
yet can not conquer,
can not merge with this,
this world of radiance and rock
and ice and shale and peace.

Myrrhina	Cease, Cretan lady, queen of the red sands and the imperious peak of Ida where Zeus reigns.
Phædra	O how I hate this world, this west, this power that strives to reach through river, town or flower, the god or spirit that inhabits it; O, is it not enough to greet the red-rose for the red, red sweet of it? must we encounter with each separate flower, some god, some goddess? must each peculiar hour, dawn, day or night, take its particular prayer? why must we pause and bear not only beauty of each beautiful thing, but suffer more, more, more; the associated spirit with its power? this tyranny of spirit that is Greece; speak, my Myrrhina, must I long endure this swarm of alien gods and this cold shore?
Myrrhina	O lady, lady, lady, luminous more than any spray of myrtle or white flower of the enchanted flowering citron-tree

that flowers and fruits
and each gleam separately,
the wax-sweet petal
by the fruit's rare gold,
listen nor count as cold
a land where purple decks your smallest
    ways,
where a king follows,
courting through long days.

Phædra

What is the dotard love
of a dull king,
Myrrhina? I know
what love might have been.

Myrrhina

O lady, lady, lady,
luminous more
than golden spray of orange
or white flower
of pearl and fire,
the citron and its leaf,
O glorious
beyond belief,
Phædra,
endure,
have strength a little more;
we shall prevail,
we will outrule this pallid shore
and sail
back to bright Crete,
its sun-lit slopes, its vales
of orange, citron,
its bright tree of myrtle;
we will escape,
radiant in all our power;
listen, endure,
O golden lily-flower.

Phædra	We all think, every one,
	sometime our power is broken,
	our fame gone,
	our beauty stricken,
	and our graciousness,
	fit only for some dark and barren place,
	where old, old women croak
	about the loom
	or pace and chatter
	graceless in the sun.
Myrrhina	Come, come,
	my lady,
	myrrh-trees bend to bless
	in Crete,
	the very foot-fall
	where you pass.
Phædra	The tall myrrh-forest
	of my distant land
	has nothing now of loveliness,
	its sand
	white and pure gold
	that drifts beneath the steps
	of the king's built-up summer palaces,
	holds no more marvellous glint,
	nor any magic
	lures me with old enchantments
	and old songs:
	O Crete shows dead and pallid
	by the flame
	and beauty
	that has given Greece its fame.
	Escape?
	escape?
	for me there is no place

can hide his fervour,
fervour of flame-lit face,
beauty as of the god that flees the sun.

Myrrhina   Dearest, my lady,
do not speak of this,
O do not breathe however faint that
    name,
peace, O my princess,
think of your great fame,
remember Crete and all those palaces,
remember all the glitter of your dead,
recall the mighty pleasaunce of the king,
your father,
and the blue, blue, of its walls,
remember Phædra is above all, all,
a queen.

Phædra   Ah, friend,
Myrrhina,
once I might have been
proud with gold head-dress
like a flame-lit flower
or candle set in some bright altar-niche;
now I am stricken
like a flame-struck bough.

Enter NURSE.

Nurse   Hist, hist my lady,
mistress, fosterling—

Phædra   What is it nurse,
what is the news you bring?

Nurse   Your lord, your very lord,
the infatuate king—

Phædra	Permits?
Nurse	—will countenance, says you may do this thing.
Phædra	O grace of wild, wild things, O swallow fair, O fair sea-swallow, flitting here and there, O swallow, beating with insatiate wing, the very pulse and centre of the air, O swallow, swallow, listening everywhere—
Myrrhina	What is this fever, this impassioned prayer?
Phædra	—you took, you severed with blue wing and fire, the very salt wind, to deliver there, back in bright Crete, my message and my prayer.
Myrrhina	Whom do you call, O mistress, by this shrine?
Phædra	I cry, I call again to her who makes the birds her message- bearer, to her who yokes the swallows to her car.

Myrrhina	She seems distraught—
	what message gave the king?

Nurse	He only granted after importunate
	prayer,
	that Phædra sleep by the cold water
	here.

Myrrhina	What—
	rest without the palace of her lord?

Nurse	Aye,
	in a tent built up of cedar-wood,
	hung over and around with canopies.

Myrrhina	What madness prompted
	these strange fantasies?

Nurse	Only despair,
	fever
	and lassitude.

Phædra	O nurse,
	O nurse,
	prepare,
	swiftly,
	the bedding,
	pillows,
	stuffed with rare
	plumes of the cygnet
	and the eider-duck;
	O nurse,
	O nurse,
	with care,
	spread the low couch
	with softest coverings,
	strip fair embroidery
	from the palace wall,

get awnings
and a carpet
of soft fleece;
spread cyclamen colour
on this icy sand,
hang curtains
vying
with the purple-fish;
make up the tent straightway;
bring the musicians,
all the singing band
of girls to stand about my tent
and keep
fever away;
at last,
at last,
I'll sleep.

Exit NURSE.

Myrrhina   Have pity,
Artemis.

Phædra   O queen
who rises regent from the sea,
I know at last
that you have answered me.

Myrrhina   O queen
who watches loyal by the coast,
tender to all the host
of desperate wandering sea-men,
lost at night,
goddess of hope and light,
guardian of vessels
broken by the storm,
see that our stricken Phædra
takes no harm.

Phædra	You call then to this pallid Delphic queen?
Myrrhina	Lady, in fear, in pain—
Phædra	Think not of her, Myrrhina, there's another—
Myrrhina	Mistress—
Phædra	—of lovers—
Myrrhina	—take care, is not this strip of sand holy and delicate, and all the reaches of this forest-land, *her* precinct?
Phædra	There is no place where my queen dare not come, tall, beautiful, of city and high wall.
Myrrhina	You dare affront this chosen sanctity?
Phædra	I'd build as often, restless, ill at ease, a small pavilion of bright stuffs and woven tapestries,

such as I've often slept in,
safe at home.

Myrrhina   That was the garden of the king your
father.

Phædra   And this the pleasaunce of the prince my
lover.

Myrrhina   You underestimate
this lady's strength—

Phædra   As you this other—

Myrrhina   O think of all her infallible strength
and pride,
queen of the deep-sea
and the implacable tide.

Phædra   And you,
of all her body frail and slender,
the grace that binds narcissus-white,
her knees,
think friend,
and ponder on her loveliness;
what, what are these,
cold and deliberate,
to her
who owns the beaked vermilion hulls,
to her,
powerful bright guardian
of the eastern sails?

Myrrhina   I tell you,
we are broken and undone.

Phædra   Nay,

my Myrrhina;
I felt
should Theseus grant this little whim,
then all were clear,
and my prayer melted him.

Myrrhina   You will betray?

Phædra   O when I see that pattern of heart's
          fervour
and his father,
I ache with some old savagery
to turn
within the heavy leaden heart
of Theseus,
some simple, fragile thing,
omnipotent,
single metal
with no flaw;
I'd turn and turn and turn
that little steel;
then, Theseus,
would you feel?

Myrrhina   What good were that,
to murder Athens' King?

Phædra   It would give me
some pleasure.

Myrrhina   O lady, turn
from this dire pondering,
look deeper, deeper,
conjure holier reasoning,
call up your soul to shun this evil
          thing;
O turn in prayer to some enchanted
          portal,

some intimate temple
set with corridor;
think how pure colour tints those sainted
    walls,
washed in and through and over
with ripe flowers,
think of the gold of saintliest lily-bud,
of lilies open like a scented cup;
O lady,
think,
pause,
pray
and conjure up
with deep emotion
and with holiest thought,
that shell of marble,
delicate temple wall;
breathe in your heart
the holiest scent of orange
that blows at noon
through those cool corridors,
some breath of citron
wafted over-seas,
imagine we were back again in Crete.

Phædra   We are, we are, Myrrhina
loveliest, hear
that voice
that answers honey-clear,
your prayer.

Boy   *Where is the nightingale,*
(sings)   *in what myrrh-wood and dim?*
O let the night come black
for we would conjure back
all that enchanted him,
    all that enchanted him.

Phædra	You see, you see, promise and prophecy.
Boy *(sings)*	*Where is the bird of fire,* *in what packed hedge of rose?* *in what roofed ledge of flower?* *no other creature knows* *what magic lurks within,* * what magic lurks within.*
Phædra	Eros speaks here, Love's child and child of fire.
Boy *(sings)*	*Bird, bird, bird, bird we cry,* *hear, pity us in pain,* *hearts break in the sunlight,* *hearts break in daylight rain,* *only night heals again,* * only night heals again.*
Phædra	Bird, bird, bird, bird we cry—

Enter BOY.

Myrrhina	Peace, lady, lady— child, what do you here?
Boy	I made a song, for the king bade me sing.

Myrrhina	But of cold mountains, of the water-fall, of lilies cold and tall—

Myrrhina

But of cold mountains,
of the water-fall,
of lilies cold and tall—

Boy

He bade me praise the queen,
his lady's rare
still beauty.

Phædra

Aye,
she is fair,
and here,
here,
here she stands.

Boy

To guide the sea-men
to this little harbour—

Phædra

Nay more—

Myrrhina

Lady beware—

Phædra

     —a prince.

Myrrhina

No—

Phædra

My waiting-lady,
my companion here,
is jealous for my safety,
for my power.

Myrrhina

Say rather,
for the duty of a queen.

Phædra

A queen,
a queen,
a queen,
O I have been

too long the mistress
of the stream and forest—

Myrrhina   Take care—

Phædra   She fears
for my high sanctity,
my holy pride,
she always watches,
always loiters near,
she and her sisters
hide about the forest,
they never leave me—

Myrrhina   Lies,
lies,
lies.

Phædra   You see,
I never meet Hippolytus
for these—

Myrrhina   Perfidious—

Phædra   —who watch
to hear and spy.

Myrrhina   O piteous wretch.

Phædra   See,
she maligns me,
she will tell you next—

Boy   What?

Phædra   This—
that I am not,

	never could be—
Myrrhina	Hi-st—
Phædra	—Artemis.
Myrrhina	O lies, O wretchedness.
Phædra	But you, you, you, I pray, I ask you this: am I, or am I not, the beauteous mistress of the haunted grot of innermost forest, queen of light and shade that flickers gold on gold, light merged with flower, flower merged with splendour of the sun's pure flame, answer and speak my name, am I the mistress and the innermost power of the pure glade!
Boy	I am afraid.
Phædra	Aye, for you see, you know that I am god, you know that I am no mortal like this other, who shrinks and fears

before Love's holiest altar,
you,
you confess
that I am Artemis.

Boy

I never yet saw,
nay,
nor met a goddess.

Phædra

But you have worshipped?

Boy

Aye,
afar.

Phædra

Where?

Boy

—in Cyprus.

Phædra

In Cyprus,
that might almost be in Crete.

Myrrhina
(to the statue)

O wild,
O fair,
O sweet,
turn back,
turn back,
beware,
evil lurks here,
evil
and traitorous pleasure.

Phædra

Say rather,
we have built here in our thought,
the very temple
that you would entreat.

Myrrhina *(to the statue)*	Lovely, O restless feet, where do you wander? where, where do you lurk? lovely, O loveliest look, look down, come soon.
Phædra	It is no use, she wanders with her brother Helios in some other world, distant and far from us— she wanders far with Helios her brother.
Myrrhina	Nay, nay but rather, lurks very near, lurks very near—
Phædra	O have no fear, Myrrhina, *she*'ll not hear.
Myrrhina	Ah, but this other—
Phædra	Has heard; heard, answered like a mystic bird, flying straight, giving spoken word—
Myrrhina	Word?
Phædra	The very song the boy has sung to us— is he not Eros?

Myrrhina	O madness, madness: cease.
Phædra	Nay, peace, assuredly no call escapes our lady, beautiful of high wall, of fortress and of every tributary—
Myrrhina	Not Delphi, not the isle Delos.
Phædra	Delphi is far, Delos is but a name.
Myrrhina	Beware—
Phædra	So sing, lad, sing again.
Boy *(sings)*	*Bring myrrh and myrtle-bud,* *bell of the snowy head* *of the first asphodel;* *frost of the citron flower,* *petal on petal, white* *wax of faint love-delight;* *flower, flower and little head* *of tiny meadow-floret,* *white, where no bee has fed;* *full of its honey yet* *spilling its scented sweet,* *spread them before her feet;*

white citron, whitest rose,
(myrrh-leaves, myrrh-leaves enclose)
and the white violet.

Myrrhina	O wicked, wicked princess.
Phædra	You see, she still demurs, is jealous—
Myrrhina	O subtle, curious lady, desperate queen—
Phædra	Ah, once I might have been desperate, flayed and hurt—
Myrrhina *(to the statue)*	Maid who enchants the host of maidens, flower of Delos, O white, white lily floating in the tide of some still inland river, frail and silver, chastity undefiled, innermost heart of sainted purity—
Phædra	Is there a thing, however white and clear, purer than fire?
Myrrhina	O mistress, mocking with your subtle tongue, be done.
Phædra	Tell to your king, your prince Hippolytus, that I *am* done,

done with my pride,
my haughty mockery,
tell him
my pleasure in this little thing,
this tiny statue that I found at dawn,
roused me
from my old poignant lethargy,
nostalgia for green things,
tree and forest,
(that witchery of wood-land
to enfold me),
that threatens to include
and draw me back,
back from holocaust of human beauty,
tell to your king,
the prince Hippolytus,
that human frailty and mortal commerce
tempt me now,
more
than any tree or forest
or any cataract
or mountain-torrent;
tell to your lord,
your prince Hippolytus
that Artemis chooses
actually as a goddess,
love, love, love, love
that mocks the lure of forests,
love that enchants the sea-fowl and the
        beast;
say,
is she least,
least of the creatures that command her
        love?
is Artemis less,
than mole
or foraging ferret?
less than the panther

than the gull or owl?
O it were ill and I were ill-advised
thus to continue lost,
alone,
no mate;
is it too late?
go ask your king,
pray piteous with my voice,
moreover—touch his soul with singing,
sing—

Boy *(sings)*	*Bring myrrh and myrtle-bud,* *bell of the snowy head* *of the first asphodel—*
Phædra	Ah that, that answers well, and any other; O make most piteous prayer, lure him with flowers—
Boy	Lady, I will.
Phædra	Aye, let him question you, say I am tall and lovely, frail, tender, and yet bold, speak of my eyes, my hands, my hair's strange, flexible texture and its gold.
Boy	Yes, I was always told the goddess

had a head-band and a dress
falling in curious folds
like this,
and curious ear-rings
and gold bracelets.

Phædra

Aye,
it is this,
this that includes me in the list of
    spirits,
only the high-born
or Olympic race
are tall and gold—

Boy
(sings)

Frost of the citron-flower,
petal on petal, white
wax of faint love-delight.

Phædra

Aye,
you are sure,
you know me,
but beware,
come secretly,
let him keep secret
all this meeting-place,
lest it be imminent death.

Myrrhina

Aye,
death were imminent—

Phædra

Let him seek out
this statue,
this still place,
just as Orion's belt shines on the water.

Boy

He shall be here.

Phædra	O queen,
(raises her arms	O bird,
in prayer	O star.
toward the sea)	

Lapse of time indicated by darkness or curtain. It is night just before dawn. The little pavilion or tent has been built up.

Voices	*Where is the nightingale,*
	in what myrrh-wood and dim?

Music continues distant.

Myrrhina	Say rather,
	where the hymn,
	the chant of maidens
	standing still and tall,
	inviolate maidens
	of chaste mien
	and all,
	all white and golden,
	like white lily flowers;
	where is the nightingale?
	nay ask,
	where,
	where the host
	and the enchanted dance?

Voices	*Where is the bird of fire,*
	in what packed hedge of rose?

Continues distant.

Myrrhina	Nay rather,
	where,
	where,

where,
perfection of those lilies,
tall and slim,
each perfect separate yet joined
again beautiful,
as separate pearls
make one whole beauty
of a diadem;
O where
the wonder
of that dance,
magic of sea and wind?

Voices   *Bird, bird, bird, bird we cry,*
hear, pity us in pain—

Distant.

Myrrhina   And I,
I cry again,
where,
where,
where
is that most sainted tread
of holy feet?
where is the dance
and the enchanted beat
that mocks the waves' enchanted
rise and fall?
where, where are all the maidens,
tenuous, slim,
like wild white lilies,
rising on tall stems?

A chorus of maidens has appeared, ghosts about the statue's plinth.

O rare perfection,
O fair,
O wild,
infinite loveliness,
O grace
and beauty.

Chorus

O love, peace,
never in any porch
or portico
can love come,
never to us,
eternal, tenuous,
who died young,
long ago,
    long ago.

Myrrhina

O beauty,
O infinite grace,
so does she come,
so does she answer us,
praying for peace.

Chorus

O love cease,
never to us at home,
guiding the lowly loom,
never to us afar,
gathering early bloom
of earthly maiden-flower,
    did love come.

Myrrhina

She speaks;
the holy lily-flower,
stripped of all passion,
tells of passion fairer—

Chorus	We are the answer,
	message-bearers,
	we answer prayer,
	ah let the night come black,
	for we have conjured back,
	her, her, her.

The ghosts fade away. The nightingale song dies down. Enter PHÆDRA
from tent.

| Phædra | Ah, |
| | it was sweet. |

Myrrhina	O lady,
	swift,
	prepare,
	prepare to flee
	this shore,
	this sanctity.

Phædra	Nay,
	I have made it mine,
	have made it Love's.

Myrrhina	Not hers,
	not hers,
	not hers.

Phædra	I say
	that I have pledged this place
	to fair
	infinite Aphrodite.

| Myrrhina | Lady, I pray |
| | come home. |

| Phædra | Home? |

Myrrhina	Back to the palace—
Phædra	Of whom?
Myrrhina	—the king.
Phædra	My king rests here.
Myrrhina	Queen, queen, beware, I have seen curious things.
Phædra	And I have felt the actual touch of wings, hers, soft, and Eros' feathers.

Enter HIPPOLYTUS *from tent.*

Hippolytus *(to the statue)*	Pardon, my thought was dark, I had forgotten quite, Latmos, your fairest hill;
	I had forsworn all joy, how could a man forget tale of your shepherd boy?
	in slight Endymion's name, turn, turn and love again for young Endymion's sake;
	by cliff, by wood and lake, by elder-grove and thicket, I sought and sought your face;

how could a mortal know
(love's meanest neophite),
that love was always near?

Phædra   Yes,
                 I am here.

Hippolytus   What do *you*
                 by this shore?

Phædra   I come like you,
                 Hippolytus,
                 for prayer.

Hippolytus   Say rather,
                 to defile a sanctity.

Phædra   Hippolytus—

Hippolytus   O what a snare,
                 a cheat—

Phædra   Hippolytus—

Hippolytus   To creep to the goddess' sanctity,
                 to spy.

Phædra   Hippolytus—

Hippolytus   I cry
                 to all the holy mountain-side—

Phædra   Hippolytus—

Hippolytus   —hear,
                 help me to avenge
                 this blasphemy.

Myrrhina	Lady, O come away.
Phædra	Hippolytus, Hippolytus, I say, I love you more, more, more (yet, is it possible?) than before.
Hippolytus	O peace, no more of all that palace-rite, that cult of incense and of tropic flowers, I say no more, no more—
Phædra	Last night—
Hippolytus	Aye, aye, aye, aye, last night—
Phædra	—I lay—
Hippolytus	—sweetly—
Phædra	from dusk almost till day—
Hippolytus	with Artemis.
Myrrhina	O do not speak,

do not speak,
mistress—

Phædra

Myrrhina,
have no fear,
I know,
I know that he lay here—

Myrrhina

—with Artemis.

Phædra

Yes,
yes,
yes,
yes,
I know,
'twas Artemis.

Hippolytus

No more
her favour,
she is gone—

Phædra

No,
no,
no,
no,
no,
no—

Hippolytus

I know that she is gone,
I know that I will never meet her
    further,
save in the storm
and in the icy river.

Phædra

No,
no,
no,

no,
say rather in some other arms,
you'll feel her shape,
that in some other form,
count her heart-beat,
so, many and many and many a one has
    found—

Hippolytus   Found infamy—

Phædra   Nay,
but a goddess in a woman's arms.

Hippolytus   Away,
and tempt me not,
for I am tired
of all this old and worn-out play,
this thread-bare plot
of love and mischief.

Phædra   Hippolytus—

Hippolytus   Cease,
go to the king,
my father.

Myrrhina   As I entreat her.

Hippolytus   She is worn out and mad—

Phædra   Nay only sad,
sad,
sad—

Hippolytus   Sadness of vile humanity;
humanity and sadness of its kind
have no place by this holy driven sea—

Phædra	Ah me—
Hippolytus	Humanity and stale and perilous lust have no place by this coast—
Phædra	Ah me—
Hippolytus	Phædra—
Phædra	My child—
Hippolytus	Not thine, not of thy king—
Phædra	Your father—
Hippolytus	And your lover—
Phædra	Pity me—
Myrrhina	O blind, infatuate—
Phædra	—'tis so with womenkind, and I was happy for a little while.
Myrrhina	O grief, O guile of love.
Phædra	For many and many and many a desolate night, I lay and tossed, ill, wan, home-sick and desperate, having foul dreams, ill thought of no good portent, O I was hopeless,

> lonely in the palace,
> bereft of friendship
> and love's loveliest solace,
> last night,
> last night,
> (O night,
> luminous with phosphorescence
> and more bright
> than day-star climbing heaven's stair
>   at noon),
> I slept.

Hippolytus

> Lady,
> I know your dream,
> I feel your thought,
> pardon my own impetuous boorishness,
> last night,
> last night, I too,
> lay bathed in phosphorescence
> like white dew.

Phædra

> Last night,
> last night,
> I slept,
> soul, body, spirit and thought.
>
> Last night,
> last night,
> it seems,
> peace came
> and dreams.

Hippolytus

> You will, I trust,
> so sleep
> for many and many
> another beauteous night.

Phædra   Not many,
Theseus' son.

Myrrhina   You are wan,
pale and blown ceaseless,
lady, by this wind,
by this sea-wind and chill,
scattering foam,
white in the dawn.

Phædra   Fasten my scarf,
straighten my comb—

Myrrhina   Ah,
you are ill—

Phædra   —for she and I
have won.

Myrrhina   Won?

Phædra   In a contest
for a prince—
with death.

Myrrhina   Not death,
not death—

Phædra   Did I say love?
did I accomplish it?

Myrrhina   Too well—

Phædra   I know how well,
for she,
she,
she has come.

Myrrhina	Lady, O lady, who? and where, where, where?
Phædra	There where the elder-blossom flecks the tide.
Myrrhina	It is sea-foam that drifts and scatters wide.
Phædra	She stands in lily-blossoms to her knees.
Myrrhina	Nay, it is froth and spindrift of the seas.
Phædra	She stands with wood-flowers wound about her head, bound with bright silver, and a silver band clasps all her kirtle, showing innocent thighs, and all her lovely features mock at me, and O her eyes, her eyes, her eyes, her eyes—
Myrrhina	O lady, lady, lady—
Phædra	—speak (for her tongue disdains), "queen,

               pitiful small queen
               and Cretan lady,
               what,
               what to mine
               is your small stricken disenchanted
                   beauty?"

Myrrhina   Come,
               come away.

Phædra   No, no, I'll stay
               forever and forever
               here.

Hippolytus   Lady,
               I was unjust and cruel
               I fear—

Phædra   Child of a king—

Hippolytus   Forgive me,
               I was wild with ecstasy.

Phædra   I will forgive
               if you make prayer for me.

Hippolytus   To whom,
               poor queen?
               what, lady,
               shall I say?

Phædra   Pray,
               pray,
               the first—

Hippolytus   *She?*

Phædra	Ah, is she ever uppermost in your thought?
Hippolytus	What would you?
Phædra	Ask another—
Hippolytus	There is no other when this one is near.
Phædra	Your mother.
Hippolytus	Hippolyta?
Phædra	For the stark beauty of the name she bore, like a bright crown or an enchanter's mitre—
Hippolytus	Hippolyta—
Phædra	—make some authentic prayer.
Hippolytus	I will entreat the water and the dawn.

Exit PHÆDRA *into tent.*

Myrrhina	The stars are almost gone.
Hippolytus	O stars drop, one, one, one by one, into the frozen rivers

or the sea,
O stars cease intimate dance,
woven with minstrelsy,
cease, cease your song;
the day is almost come;
O stars,
so pale,
after your night of joy
and ecstasy.

Myrrhina   The dawn—

Hippolytus   O dawn
arise,
leave your low couch
and shine
across the world,
give every Grecian city
light, invoke
on each tall hill
the tallest ash or pine,
shine,
and resplendent cast
the stars
into the water;
have you need of gems
after a night
so luminous
with dreams?

Myrrhina   She comes—

Hippolytus   And now,
wandering o'er the cliff,
her shoes take fire,
her sandals,
sewn with pearl,

cold in the dew,
are riven and inset
with fire-opal;
O dawn,
now you have come,
you bring a message;
in your hands a phial
of distilled dew
of healing,
in your wings,
fragrance and light
of rose
and alabaster.

O dawn,
pour
peace of holy healing,
rain your power
across the islands
and the Grecian water.

Myrrhina　　　　And you,
(to the statue)　　lady,
　　　　　　　　O lady of this loveliest sand,
　　　　　　　　pity and understand.

Silence and short pause. MYRRHINA *looks around in sudden apprehension.*

Phædra　　　　Aye,
(from within　　aye,
tent)　　　　　　aye,
　　　　　　　　aye,
　　　　　　　　aye,
　　　　　　　　aye,
　　　　　　　　pity me,
　　　　　　　　pity me,

pity me,
and draw near.

*Lapse of time indicated by darkness or curtain. It is day. The little
pavilion or tent has been removed. Enter* HYPERIDES.

Hyperides	What do you here?
Hippolytus	I offer in this dazzling day, fresh prayer.
Hyperides	Prayer?
Hippolytus	For that sick lady there.
Hyperides	Lady— to whom then, do your words refer?
Hippolytus	For Phædra who lies ill there, in the tent.
Hyperides	Gods, are you mad? you meant—
Hippolytus	Meant?
Hyperides	Prayer for the Cretan princess, Athens' queen, Phædra, no more an exile on this shore.
Hippolytus	Dead?

Hyperides   Were you then so intent
            upon your prayer,
            your worship of this chaste
            and distant lady
            that you did not see
            that other,
            broken,
            in her death so still,
            that body wan and white
            as scattered foam,
            they draped in purple
            and took reverently—

Hippolytus   Where?

Hyperides   Back to her lord,
            Theseus,
            veiled and slight,
            wan as a bride
            within her bridal chamber.

Hippolytus   Ah,
            I remember.

Hyperides   Come,
            come,
            my prince,
            surely—

Hippolytus   Yes,
            I remember,
            she was white and fair,
            and I, I
            rested with my lady there—

Hyperides   Hi-st—

Hippolytus	In a bright tent, built up of fragrant cedar.
Hyperides	Not *here?*
Hippolytus	Aye, but it's gone, the whole thing was a dream; so gods are wont to show on earth their splendour, stooping to mortals, and so disappear—
Hyperides	My lord Hippolytus, attend— you are struck mad, blinded with your old fever, the king allowed last night, by some bad error, the queen to sleep here by this frozen shore; the servants of the queen built up a tent, circled it with rare flowering bush of myrtle; her girls sang here.
Hippolytus	No, no, no, no, no, no, *that* was a dream.

Hyperides	A dream?
Hippolytus	The tent, the flowering plants, the myrrh in baskets, the myrtle-trees that stood there.
Hyperides	My prince, it was a very plausible fact, only the king regrets—
Hippolytus	Regrets?
Hyperides	That he gave in to that strange fantasy of Phædra.
Hippolytus	Fantasy?
Hyperides	That she should rest afar out of the palace, aye, even from the garden and her favourite fountain and sleep here.
Hippolytus	Hyperides, you jest—
Hyperides	I jest?
Hippolytus	Unspeakable untimely jeer—
Hyperides	Ah, if it were—
Hippolytus	Myself, Hyperides,

I lay within this tent,
myself, I slept,
held close—

Hyperides   Tell not this thing—

Hippolytus   To you,
to you, I tell
how secretly,
how exquisitely
I was favoured—

Hyperides   No more—

Hippolytus   —of *her*.

Hyperides   Alas,
alas,
'twas Phædra.

Hippolytus   No,
no,
no,
no,
you err.

Hyperides   Prince, you are mad
and Phædra is your mother—

Hippolytus   Aye, like Hippolyta
and this one, this other—

Hyperides   You fool.

Hippolytus   Fool?

Hyperides   She worked on you
with diabolic power,

offered mayhap
some cup,
engendered with those Cretan serving-
    girls,
some charm,
something,
some evil
from her perilous east,
and harm.

Hippolytus   There was no charm,
no diabolic cup,
only the peace
and favour of the goddess.

Hyperides   Come,
come
and summon all your memory,
come prince and king,
arise from this dark sloth,
wake up.

Hippolytus   I am awake,
stark and alert,
and O, her hands
were cool.

Hyperides   Listen,
my pitiful friend—

Hippolytus   The end
was beautiful.

Hyperides   You are distraught
by Phædra's death.

Hippolytus   How died she then?

Hyperides   O,
a most pitiful end.

Hippolytus   Speak on.

Hyperides   The silken tassels of her girdle swung
from the tent-pole,
there Phædra hung awhile and cried
most piteously,
aye,
aye,
aye,
aye,
aye,
aye,
pity me,
pity me,
pity me,
and draw near.

Hippolytus   How did you hear
this thing?

Hyperides   From her nurse
and Myrrhina—

Hippolytus   Then it is really over?

Hyperides   Phædra lies
covered with myrtle flowers
and the death purple.

Hippolytus   How was it that I missed all this?
you see obviously your tale is crass
      invention
and you lie.

Hyperides	Nay, king, you were intent, they say, embraced the white plinth of the goddess here, deep, deep in intimate prayer.
Hippolytus	I slept, perhaps.
Hyperides	Yes, mercifully bereft of knowledge of this strange and hideous end.
Hippolytus	By *this* white sand.
Hyperides	Yes, by the goddess' shrine.
Hippolytus	But she, how came that amorous queen to choose *this* place?
Hyperides	They say, stricken with fever, hot and hot and hot, she sought the cleansing tide and prayed the goddess.
Hippolytus	Ah, you *have* lied.
Hyperides	Lied?
Hippolytus	You say the queen was hot, again was stricken, burnt and burning away, but I, I say

that thing that held me
was a broken bird,
with arms cold like a sea-gull from the
    sea,
I say (and I repeat) those hands were
    cold,
and O, the white was luminous
and not mortal,
and no mortal gold
was that gold lock
that slid across my eyes.

Hyperides

Listen, my prince,
all my intent to save
were traitorous toward Athens' king,
I must speak out,
speak truth
for your sake,
for the sake of that lost queen,
tell no one,
no one,
no one
of this thing—

Hippolytus

One does not speak
save to an intimate—

Hyperides

Speak to no intimate even,
speak to none—

Hippolytus

Yes,
it were wrong,
for that love
was no evanescent thing,
nor that a mortal.

O cold, O listless wing—

she lay as a bird broken
by wind strength,
and had no power to raise
a head that faltered like a broken
    flower;
she had no power to lift
a head gone listless
on its flower stalk;
she could not move nor walk;
O goddess,
child-like
and so pitiful,
you,
all so swift and wild and beautiful,
you all so strong, so fearless,
never tired
of following the wild things on the
    hill,
how could you lie so still?

How could I tell,
tell anyone of this,
this goddess swept here,
like a wind-swept gull?

Call me my steeds,
is there a mortal yet
arises
after resting with a goddess,
other than wild and passionate and
    glad,
bring me my steeds,
my champing ones,
my chariot.

Hyperides   King,
you are over-wrought and wild and see
the wind howls ominously.

Hippolytus	Aye, after such a night of star and gold, the wind drives cold.
Hyperides	See how the spray is sweeping from the sea—
Hippolytus	As snow blown from the peak of some tall tree—
Hyperides	Hear how the wind is whipping up the sand—
Hippolytus	As silver and as white as her head-band—
Hyperides	Hear how the tide moans perilously along—
Hippolytus	As low, as soft, as ominous as her song.

Call me my chariot,
I would flout the waves
and still my gladness,
lest I tell this thing
to all the Athenians,
shouting riotous.

ACT III

The same strip of seacoast. HIPPOLYTUS *lies where he has been flung from his chariot, at the base of the statue. Enter* HELIOS.

Helios　　　**I,**
　　　　　　I who lead the sea-men on the ship,
　　　　　　telling my will by dolphin
　　　　　　or bright gull,
　　　　　　sending the softest wind
　　　　　　to waft ashore
　　　　　　those who implore my guidance
　　　　　　and my piloting at night,
　　　　　　I,
　　　　　　I who sent aright
　　　　　　but lately one bright sail
　　　　　　to Syracuse,
　　　　　　returning to this shore
　　　　　　to turn about
　　　　　　another floundering,
　　　　　　and to waft another
　　　　　　beyond pro-pontis
　　　　　　into quiet water,
　　　　　　I,
　　　　　　while I stilled the gale
　　　　　　and kept the sea silent with my
　　　　　　　　　enchantment,
　　　　　　heard
　　　　　　even while I loitered
　　　　　　by this salty reef,
　　　　　　this,
　　　　　　(that sundered all my will
　　　　　　from sail and shoal),
　　　　　　Artemis,
　　　　　　Artemis,
　　　　　　Artemis,
　　　　　　Artemis.

Hippolytus	Artemis, Artemis, Artemis, Artemis.
Helios	She is the help of huntsmen who invoke her aid in searching out the pleasant lair of the hill-lion fathering his whelps, of fox and lynx and panther and wild bear; she is the friend of huntsmen who implore her aid in snaring snipe or water-fowl, she answers when the lowliest fisher calls, seeking her help to net the clumsy school of leaping wrasse or blue-fish or white tunny; she knows the haunt even of the finny tribe who leap the wave-crest silently or seek in the cave depth their shelter, or else hide under the lee-side of the weedy rock, she knows the shell-fish burrowing in the sand,

seeking the wash and shelter of the
tide.

Hippolytus   Artemis,
Artemis,
Artemis,
Artemis.

Helios   So,
since none hide,
since none escape her eyes,
vigilant huntress,
pilot and ships' guide,
since none, none, none
escape her luminous feet,
since no bird falters
that she does not seek
either to shelter,
loosening from the trap,
or to grant
sudden, painless and swift death,
how,
since her feet run to untrap the fowl,
taken too soon,
with birdlets
left to die,
does she whose eyes
penetrate lair and hollow,
the sea-crest and the hill-crest
and the shallow
gold and white streamlet
hastening to the bay,
how,
how does she delay,
while this faint breath
even while it falters,
summons
Artemis?

Hippolytus	Artemis, Artemis, Artemis, Artemis.
Helios	O white, O luminous maid, have the wild hills provoked a blame so sure, a shame so perilous? for how could you ignore one made so piteous, broken by your snare? following your beauty he was dazed and fell down the precipitous shelf, or some beast tore this huntsman lying broken on the shore; lady, O turn, I, I, I, I implore; shall base men desecrate Delphi? shall Delos' mart excel its fane and the merchant the old temple worshipper?
Hippolytus	Artemis, Artemis, Artemis, Artemis.

Helios	O pause, pause, pause and press
	your own white glaive
	into that snow of breast,
	teach us who doubt
	that you have god-like veins,
	that you too beat
	to joy and ecstasy,
	O must I think that you are some
	    cold sprite,
	some demon of ill nature
	and small spite?
	must I then say you are not beautiful?
	what high enchantment of the mountain
	    shale
	teaches that man is less,
	less than the sea-swept rock
	or windy cliff?

Hippolytus	Artemis, Artemis, Artemis, Artemis—
Helios	O turn, O turn and bless this stricken form, these whitest hands that yearn, yearn upwards toward your snow-encrusted thickets, O turn, turn, hesitate, place cold snow on this fevered brow and limbs, burnt with despair; O beautiful,

stark,
glittering,
spirit of light and air,
have you no pity,
no heart anywhere?

Hippolytus   Artemis,
            Artemis,
            Artemis,
            Artemis—

Enter ARTEMIS.

Helios   O Delian lady,
            pillaging afar
            the slopes of Pelion
            for the spotted deer,
            how can you be so fair?
            how can you be so wild and beautiful
            and yet so heartless?
            how,
            how could you bear
            to track the red-fox
            to his cavernous lair?
            how could you follow
            the lynx,
            the wild-cat
            and the lordlier panther,
            spurning this stricken prey,
            calling you here?

Hippolytus   Artemis,
            Artemis,
            Artemis—

Helios   O,
            O thou heartless,

O thou passionless maid,
O you should fly
as some insidious plague
the tyrannous green-wood
and its poisonous shade
that works like some still poison
in the blood,
until men turn and hate
the city portal
and the city gate,
until they shun as ill
all, all man's wisdom,
all art's subtleties,
and worship and call good
only the haunted shade
of the dark wood.

Hippolytus   Artemis,
                Artemis—

Artemis   Silence then both of you
                with your indictments
                and your tyrannies,
                how can you judge the true,
                the upright,
                righteous
                or the holy man?
                how can you know
                what hindered,
                what prevented
                or what span
                of severing sea divided?
                am I a mortal
                or some fickle maid
                that you must rail,
                must summon,
                must acclaim me cruel?

what do you know,
what feel?
O but speak not,
I know
from long and bitter intimacy
what you,
O king,
will say.

Helios

What can I speak,
what is there left to say,
O Delian lady,
clambering the height
of mountains,
searching levels of the shore,
following the sea-tide with the glimmering
     fish,
guardian of sea-men,
present help to guide
the fisher
struggling with the shoal and tide,
O Delphian,
ever present help,
saviour and guardian,
what,
what can I say,
what can I ask,
but how,
how missed you this?

Artemis

O Delphian,
high enchanter
and arch-mage,
O prophet,
O harp-player,
O most sage
giver of wisdom,

maker of the seven
most potent sayings
that the ears of men
(not yet initiate
to godly rite),
may hear,
may speak,
may ponder,
yet retain sanity,
even their mortality,
nor break,
stricken and riven
by your holy flame,
O king,
O great,
whose name
the distant Lydians
and near isles acclaim,
judge me
and hate.

Helios

O Delian,
O most beautiful,
most fleet,
O words that fly
like winged things,
flying late
back to the sand
and sand-dunes of the south,
O chaste,
O scornful mouth,
O heaven's beauty,
holy maidenhood,
O fair and good,
O Delian,
white like flame,
what is it?

what acclaim is lacking?
tell me what altar
lacks its altar-cake?
tell me what temple
has neglected you,
and I shall rise,
(whether it be far Scythia
or near isle),
and I shall plague that people
with dire plague
of fire
or dearth of water.

Artemis   Most imminent pest—
naught can dispel that plague.

Helios   What rends you,
what distresses you, proud maid?

Artemis   A plague has entered,
taken of my best.

Helios   Speak, tell me what affliction,
I will heal.

Artemis   Not even you, Pæon,
can cleanse this ill.

Helios   Spirit of Delos,
you ignore my fame.

Artemis   But none, none, none
dare flaunt that spirited name.

Helios   Speak, speak that name
and I will cope with it.

Hippolytus	Artemis, Delian Artemis, your kiss—
Artemis	Beware, beware words, subtle and so far—
Hippolytus	I breathe in pain, in pain, with little breath—
Artemis	Words deadly, deadly as the viper's kiss—
Hippolytus	Your kiss, Artemis, Artemis, your kiss—
Artemis	In this, this place inviolate and blest?
Hippolytus	Love makes more sure, more sacred, holy things—
Artemis	O cruel, bitter, cruel, insatiate queen—
Helios	Who is this queen, cruel and insatiable?
Artemis	Invidious and helpless with white doves—
Hippolytus	Fair—fair—her doves drew here her fiery car—
Artemis	Silence—no more—no more— no more—no more—
Helios	Speak one of you, explain this curious thing—

Artemis	Treachery unspeakable and perjury—
Helios	I will be fair, I will sift wrong from right—
Artemis	There is no right where all is basely done—
Helios	Your desperate plight—say lad, what caused it then?
Hippolytus	Love sank a moment, listless after flight—
Artemis	Love seized and like a ravaging hawk, tore outright—
Hippolytus	Love hovered till his wings brushed all my soul—
Artemis	Love took rapacious and devoured whole—
Hippolytus	Love reconciled the cold hills to the stars—
Artemis	Love scorched the thickets and destroyed the flowers—
Hippolytus	Love stood and with his sandals trod like wine—
Artemis	He fouled and trampled all my fair white shrine—
Hippolytus	—my heart, till ecstasy and intoxicant—

Artemis   —and blasphemed
                    all this holy shore of mine—

Hippolytus   —filled with its fervour
                    my enchanted spirit—

Artemis   —till it is threatened
                    and no more my own—

Hippolytus   —and all my soul was lifted
                    as with wine—

Artemis   —but desperate
                    that shone so fair and pure—

Hippolytus   —and all my spirit
                    and my soul were joined—

Artemis   —and the wild beauty now
                    is gone from here—

Hippolytus   —forever and forever
                    with my veins—

Artemis   —and all the sanctity
                    and holiest grace—

Hippolytus   —my flesh, my hands, my feet—
                    all, all was spirit—

Helios   O god and mortal cease.

Enter BOY, *not perceiving the group.*

Boy   There is no town in Greece
                    ignores his fame,
                    there is no fane
                    in island

or the furtherest sands
but chants his name,
there is no temple,
but red-hyacinth and cyclamen
frame
a crown
on the white altar; no man stands
with comfortless hands;
none pray him but he sends
answer,
none turn away
with empty hands.

Artemis   O destiny—

Boy   There is no star
that may ignore his fire,
no altar burns
but he claims share
of every hecatomb;
he knows the blinding desert
and the strands,
pale in the noon-day,
parched and comfortless,
he heals all thirst;
he knows the lands
that claim the northern crown
and none go down
into the avid sea
but he accounts,
saves,
yea and spares.

Helios   O ecstasy—

Boy   There are no tears
that his fire does not heal,

no fears
driving the herdsman
gathering his sheep,
the sailor with the stars,
the merchant in the desert,
but he hears,
none, none may pray too late,
for he even at the last
remains, when all the gods are silent
and forsake
altar and worshippers.

He turns.

Artemis   What do you here?

Boy   I come after night's ecstasy,
for prayer.

Artemis   Do you not know?
did you not hear?

Boy   I heard the linnets
in the woods above.

Artemis   Did you not hear
the treachery of Love?

Boy   I heard the plover
following the gull.

Artemis   Do you not see Death
hovering for this soul?

Boy   Alas—alas—
my prince—Hippolytus—

Artemis	He lies here shattered by his broken car—
Boy	O loveliest—Athens' loveliest lost star—
Artemis	O body stricken, heart and soul undone—
Boy	O being whole, now finished and made one—
Artemis	One, one in body, broken in his soul—
Boy	His soul is welded in ecstatic heat—
Helios	His hands are broken and those beauteous feet—
Artemis	His heart is taken and his soul is gone—
Boy	His hands and side blossom with holy wound—
Artemis	His soul and body are broken and defamed—
Boy	His soul is beautiful in Love's great name—
Artemis	His body pallid, wan and without fame—
Boy	His body bright with red and luminous blood—

Artemis	His body is disgraced by treacherous love—
Boy	His body blossoms as Adonis did—
Artemis	He has no place now in my sacred grove—
Boy	He shows more holy for the stain of love—
Artemis	No host of lilies by the Delian tree—
Boy	He has a place, fair in infinity—
Artemis	He has no place where any god may come—
Helios	He has his home forever, in white song—
Artemis	I speak and cast away all claim of his—
Helios	You are less strong, O Delian, than love—
Artemis	O desecration and unhappiness—
Helios	O exquisite consummation and sheer bliss—
Artemis	Song, song, song, song it is that shatters all—

Helios	Song, song, song baffles the fears of death—
Artemis	Then is all, all forgiven in song's name—
Helios	All, all lost beauty shelters in its fane—
Boy	He dies, he falls, fainting with little breath—
Helios	Hippolytus, O fair, O beauteous name—
Boy	He calls, O lady, hear Hippolytus—
Helios	O evil fate, O dire O hapless deed—
Artemis	O evil deed, O dire, O hapless fate—
Boy	Speak, comfort him, he calls—he calls—
Artemis	—too late.
Boy	Alas, alas, I go, I haste to bring the Trœzians who may yet prevent this thing

Exit BOY.

Hippolytus *(stands)*	O beauty of the marble altar base, O land I must forsake, Athens—
Artemis	He calls now to the city of his birth—
Hippolytus	O halls and haunts of mirth, O citizens laughing and with quiet hands, bring one and all, all to this citadel—
Helios	Befriend him lest he fall—
Hippolytus	—the violets of her beauty, and all, all the lilies brightening the fields in all, all Attica, in every deme—
Artemis	For whom? who then?
Hippolytus	For her who stands beside the fountains with her brother—
Artemis	For us— for us—
Hippolytus	—and from all, all the distant other-lands, roses in pious hands.

HIPPOLYTUS *falls forward.*

Artemis	Now he has taken what my flame
	would spare;
	white crystal of pure water
	has more power
	than blinding golden fire,
	yet he has taken,
	winnowing the air,
	polluted what was fair.
Helios	None may affront his name,
	not one of us,
	ah cruel Eros,
	none may dispel the gloom
	that his name tells,
	all, all must fail,
	thou, I and luminous God;
	Eros is still man's tyrant
	and god's king;
	O queen of Delphi,
	O white powerful flame,
	has he then spoken,
	has he said your name?
	has he, the least,
	O very greatest one,
	affronted you
	and shamed?
Artemis	No, no, O king,
	O prophet,
	O harp-player,
	mage and the first
	giver of wisdom,
	Love has not vanquished,
	has not stricken me,
	Love has not stayed my wild feet
	from the hills
	nor made me shudder,

glad and white and still,
no song of his
lured me
with poignant note;
no shrill song-note
of mine
responded to his piercing flute;
no,
I was mute.

Helios   Then sister,
O beloved,
O most fair,
why do you shiver?
why, why rend the air
with such a face,
uplifted and so white?
no god has yet seen
nay nor borne
so bright
a diadem,
wrought with so clear a gem,
no, no god wears
so white a circlet
as that bright one there,
that stark pain
that your stricken forehead
bears.

Artemis   O bright,
O gold,
O king of mysteries
and mystic rite,
O Delphic ruler
of high-priest and white
wan and forsaken Pythian,
you,

you who know
the mysteries beyond death
and before,
speak,
is there one,
one that is more
more tyrannous,
more treacherous
than life?

Helios

O white enchantress,
O white lily-bud,
O head so golden,
none such holy brood
did ever white swan
breed beside a river,
nor has God ever
begotten near his throne-room
in high heaven
such, such—
not even the seven Pleiads,
all, all seven
shine like you,
sternly proud;
O virgin, bright, unbroken,
what, what has threatened
if it is not Love?

The chorus of maidens appears, ghosts encircling the body of HIPPOLYTUS.
They dance about the plinth of the statue.

Chorus

O love cease,
never in porch or corridor
does love come,
never to us,
eternal, tenuous,
who died young,

long ago,
> *long ago.*

Artemis

O peace,
O slow and stately posture,
O pure fire,
thus,
thus do my attendants come,
seeking the soul.

Chorus

Never to us,
never to us,
did love come,
never to us who strove,
threading the loom,
never to us who sought
dawn and noon,
flame of white flower
whose fire is purer
> *than love.*

Helios

O stately pause,
O royal diadem,
no queen has ever known
so proud,
so stainless and so rare a crown
as this fair ring,
your maidens
who attend you
and who sing.

Chorus

Never to us apart
did love thwart
body and soul and mind
with poisonous dart,
searing our happiness,
marring content,
> *tearing the heart.*

Helios	True, you are right, there is an ecstasy in hope, in these still forms, in this stern dance, in pious feet.
Chorus	*Never, O never roam,* *naming her sweet,* *never invoke,* *never entreat* *her the dark passion-flower* *treading the foam.*
Helios	Yet is it just? so dear a body lost? so fair, so young, is he yet gone?
Chorus	*Come,* *come to Delos,* *follow us home,* *arise, arise, let us* *over the foam,* *sing and give answer,* *for life is done.*
Helios	Who says that life is done? who names the soul's going? who times the coming of the soul but she?
Chorus	*Never, O never,* *wandering from home,*

ask of another,
"how did love come?
what is love, sister?
what has he done?"
peace, O my dear ones,
        questioning none.

Helios   Nay,
              nay,
              be gone,
              I feel the web,
              the ecstasy, the lure
              of peace,
              the power
              that negates life,
              be off,
              I see,
              I see
              the snare.

Chorus   *Soul, soul, O deathless,*
              soul, soul, O come,
              come, come to Delos,
              rest and be done,
              done with all passion
                    pure and alone.

Helios   None, none is pure,
              and none, none is alone,
              be off,
              be gone—

The CHORUS *fades away.*

Artemis   King,
              king,
              what have you done?

Helios   Am I,
                      I,
                      Pæon
                      in vain?

Artemis   None may thwart death—

Helios   But one—

Artemis   But see,
                      his face is white,
                      deep-purple rims his eyes,
                      his pain is gone,
                      his hands are quiet,
                      all his beauty dies
                      like a parched hyacinth.

Helios   Do all the isles
                      acclaim me?
                      am I master,
                      lord, magician, sage?
                      tell, tell me,
                      you are tranced and still
                      though you must know
                      I am more powerful
                      than heaven's will
                      and death must pause
                      and death must stand amazed
                      even at the life,
                      the strength my hands distil,
                      the spark electric
                      that bids sick arise
                      and dead men falter
                      groping toward the tomb,
                      peace sister,
                      come,
                      have faith in my great mastery,
                      be strong.

Artemis

O king,
king cease,
he is already dead
and gone to Death,
my soul, my soul, my soul
and all the blest host of immortals
must acclaim him now;
he is gone white,
his brow glazed over
like some restless pool
when ice glazes a surface
that has beat the shore,
gone restful now and clear.

Helios

Then,
is my fame
so small a thing
that all the altars burn
from Didymus
even to the foaming straits?
am I the king of Delphi
and the isle
that shines like one white petal on the
    sea,
Delos,
and of the distant tributary
of golden Asia
and of India's lore?
tell me,
am I the lord of far rare herbs
that heal,
fair branch and bark,
precious from Syria?
am I, I lord of healing,
Pæon, more—master of spirit,
king of the white fire
that summons mortals
even beyond Styx?
what do you fear?

Artemis	How can I know if it be love or death?
Helios	Shall death spoil and shall love spoil, and we stand and gape here speechless as at naught at all? are we then slaves? where is your kingdom, where your fire? Death has insulted our divinity and Love has stolen: shall we stand speechless, impotent nor move? nay, nay O good and queenly lady; no tears fall but bitter pain sears all your stricken beauty: men may stand by and look and say half pitiful, "a goddess grieves," not I, not I, not I—
Artemis	We are not always powerful, O king of heaven; once, once in Sparta an iron-disc was driven straight by the wind against an innocent brow, and now

that name flowers by the water,
blooms upon the shelves,
its passionate letters
flame beneath our feet,
crying *aie, aie* forever,
its scented bells
wave and distil
pure incense
like white dew,
so cold, so sweet, so new,
and yet so old,
so old
and comfortless.

Helios

O maid so blest,
what is it you reveal?
peace, peace,
what would you tell?
my heart is stricken
by that flower-name,
that name is spoken
and I am a flame,
blown heedless in the wind,
I move and breathe
sparsely,
my own heart,
god-like and so bold,
fails in its beat,
it beats uncertainly,
my pulse fails,
I grow cold;
what do you hint?
why,
why recall this thing?

Artemis

As that one flames
immortal on the hills,
let this one still

stand by each harbour,
by each estuary
where ships beach
by the tiny wharf or quay,
a symbol of my love,
an emissary
of faith
and friendship
between god and man.

Helios   Nay,
I embraced a flower
and it was chill,
and it was cold,
and O no bitterness
can equal that keen sorrow
that I had;
ah piteous lad,
I will spare you that grandeur
of the hills,
that purity
and nullity of flowers,
arise and stand.

Artemis   And I would keep him
sacred and apart,
and I would have him
chill against my heart,
I, I would cherish,
I would shelter him
turned to a spirit,
holy in my court,
I, I would set him
against Delian marble,
whiter than all,
all the white pillars
of that corridor.

Helios   But I,
I will another thing,
I cry
to all the old dark magic of the seas,
to alter-conjurations beneath waves,
to palace and to blinding corridor
in Egypt,
further,
to most distant Asia,
to tributaries
where my kingship fills
the heart of priest
and devote with white fire
so that they burn
desiring death,
knowing there is no help,
no escape other
from my white passion,
my magician's fire;
by all that know me,
all that hold my name
for what it is,
love, god's most passionate flame,
Anax, immortal,
come,
call,
call to Pæon, power
beyond man's thought
or gods' imagining,
listen,
invoke, ye priests
and citizens
initiate to my rite,
myself again,
myself,
distant,
intense
dispassionate flame.

> Come,
> Pæon,
> Pæon,
> Power,
> myself but beyond shape
> of god or man,
> come then Myself
> abstraction, mystic fire,
> lift up,
> lift up,
> as a sun-ray may lift
> from a dank marsh,
> a broken flower.

HIPPOLYTUS *stirs.* ARTEMIS *kneels supporting him.*

Hippolytus	Love, you have changed your dress—
Artemis	Child, child—
Hippolytus	This is so white; where is the hem of little budding flowers, the purple stitches and the tiny gems, sewn in the girdle?
Artemis	Is this not beautiful?
Hippolytus	You always were, but not so kind as now, just now— how was it— all, all the roses of all other lands lost colour,

all, all the strands
that bound your head-band
were of purple,
dark purple threads
that bound
the darker purple
of Adonis-flowers,
wound in a chaplet;
all, all the roses
of all other lands
lost colour;
and the sands
burnt where you trod—

Artemis   O treacherous god—

Hippolytus   Nay,
nay,
my sweet,
he was not treacherous,
he found me, led me,
brought me to your feet—

Artemis   Not mine,
not mine,
not mine.

Hippolytus   Then whose?
but why so shine,
why shine so white,
so cold, so luminous,
who were but now so soft,
so covered
with small flowers—

Artemis   Nay, peace—

Hippolytus	Your wings were beating all the perilous night, I heard Death come but I did not take fright, your feet were fire and cyclamen your clothes, your robe was purple, your bright diadem rose, your feet were luminous as a riven flame, Goddess, O deathless name—
Artemis	O flame, perfidious—
Hippolytus	Nay, sweet, nay, cold and fair, all, all the air, acclaimed you, all the stars hung silent as we passed; you held me close; I breathed the breath of rose; I could not see your eyes, so sweet, so kind, I feared to face you openly in the wind that tossed about us, beating to drive us back, beating to suffocate and vanquish us; not that—not that— no evil Boreas, no fickle west wind, nay nor south could check your beautiful will, we soared up like a cloud and fell—

Artemis	Fell where?
Hippolytus	Far from this coast.
Artemis	He is thrice-lost.
Hippolytus	O Love, Love, Love afar, no mountain shelter blossoming with wild-flower, with lily splendour, with the summer elder, no mountain path, no peak that breaks the azure as some tall pillar slung across with colour, embroidered with bright gold of fir-branch or the slender limb of the birch with under-leaf of silver, no peak, no mountain and no icier shale beyond, edged with wild crocus, not the glacial splendour forgets, is lost, exists without Love's altar.
Artemis	All, all is broken by her treachery.
Hippolytus	*Where is the nightingale?* I know for I have seen

his very ledge of fire,
have dared desire,
am broken by his flame;
where is the bird of fire?
I know—
in a far palace,
in an orange glade.

Artemis	Pæon, O see, his mind is changed with rapture, this is not the Hippolytus of old.

Hippolytus	Gold, gold, gold, gold her feet, her hands are ivory and sweet, sweet, sweet her breath, the orange and the quince invented it, rare, rare her feet, her hands equable and cool, her body tall, tall, tall, only a slight smooth sapling which a fall of snow has bent and conquering, left.

Artemis	I am bereft.

Hippolytus	Cold, cold her exquisite feet—

Artemis	Whom does he call, O king, whom does he seek?

Hippolytus	Cold, cold, cold, cold and wild, and no lost child could cling to my arms, and no broken nestling find shelter as she found.
Artemis	Now he is lost and I am comfortless.
Hippolytus	Tide nears the full— rose-laurel trees throw purple shadow—
Artemis	Tell me, O where, where, where?
Hippolytus	In Cyprus.
Artemis	See, he is gone, is lost, has thwarted us.
Hippolytus	Goddess, my queen, a kiss.

ARTEMIS *kisses him.*

Artemis	Let him go back to death.

Enter BOY, *followed by* HYPERIDES *and the huntsmen.*

Boy	Here, here he lies.
Hyperides	Alas, torn by the chariot, broken by the tide.

Exit with the dead body of HIPPOLYTUS.

Helios	Again I fail, Again I fail to prove my absolute, my passionate love for her who walks as star-dust, Phosphoros, blown at night, across high perilous frontiers of the north, who treads as sea-foam, even the perilous seas, splendour of Erymanthus and its light, O queen of Delos, queen of my high towers even at Delphi, hail, hail and farewell.

Exit HELIOS.

Artemis	I heard the intolerable rhythm and sound of prayer, I must be hidden where no mortals are, no sycophant of priest to mar my ease; climbing impassible stairs

of rock
and forest shale
and barriers of trees:

someone will come
after I shun each place
and set a circle,
blunt end up,
of stones,
and pile an altar,
but I shall have gone
further,
toward loftier barrier,
mightier trees;
bear, wolf and pard
I will entice with me,
that eyes' black fire
or yellow,
flatter,
conjure,
feed desire,
conspire,
lead me yet further
to some loftier shelf,
untrodden;
unappeased,
I will disport at ease
and wait;
I will engage in thought and plot with
    earth
how we may best efface
from Elæa
and all stony Peloponnese,
from wild Arcadia,
from the Isthmian straits,
from Thrace and Locrian hills,
(as isles are sunk

in overwhelming seas),
all Grecian cities
with the wild arbutus
and the luminous trees.

NOTE ON THE TEXT

THE TEXT of this edition of *Hippolytus Temporizes* incorporates the emendations made by H. D. in 1955 in a copy of the 1927 printing (published by Houghton Mifflin) given to Norman Holmes Pearson and now in the Collection of American Literature, Beinecke Rare Book and Manuscript Library, Yale University (whose helpful and courteous staff are all to be thanked). In one of the drafts for "Compassionate Friendship," H. D. noted: "Today, Saturday [Feb. 26, 1955], I read through *Hippolytus Temporizes*, making many corrections, chiefly commas. . . . I must have begun work on it, then, just about 30 years ago."

In the same draft, H. D. wrote of the play:

> The stanzas and lines run on and into the infinite—realized by rock and shale and snow and wind and foam and storm. I was realizing a self, a super-ego, if you will, that was an octave above my ordinary self—and fighting to realize it. Once the poem was created, this world was created, I had to come back, to return to the ordinary things. I am tremendously touched by the play and admire it, technique and subject matter. But how did I write it?

The writing of *Hippolytus Temporizes* overlapped both H. D.'s concluding work on *Palimpsest* (1926) and her beginning *Hedylus* (1928)—all of whose themes are interconnected. The following isolated fragments indicate lines scored in the margin by H. D. during her 1955 reading of the play and present a mosaic of its themes.

ACT I

Hippolytus   . . . no tenderness can keep you
in God's palace . . .

Artemis   Gods may not
cut athwart
a mortal's fate.

Hippolytus	. . . her white soul is my strength . . .
Artemis	. . . valiant and fervid amazon is dead.
Hippolytus	. . . seek only a little further.
Artemis	Tempt not the gods—
Artemis	. . . the woods are mine but not the hearts of kings.
Hyperides	. . . this boy infatuation for a wraith . . .
Hyperides	Queen, goddess, sorceress.
Hyperides	. . . you are the victim of some evil charm or devil magic.
Hippolytus	My mind is well enough in solitude.
Hippolytus	. . . how gladly will this place be joyous witness of blood-sacrifice.
Hippolytus	. . . the perfect servant of the imperfect prince.
Hippolytus	. . . queen only of the soul, white Artemis.

Hippolytus	. . . burning with vivid brilliance . . .
Hippolytus	Hyperides, whose name might fire and blaze and gleam . . .
Boy	. . . I am reminded of the drowning men—
Hippolytus	. . . what is your reason to this wild unrest?
Hippolytus	What is song for, what use is song at all . . .
Hyperides	Song is a thing, fitted to time and measure.
Hippolytus	O I am tired and weary in the day, the night was long . . .

ACT II

Phædra	. . . this tyranny of spirit that is Greece . . .
Phædra	. . . the very pulse and centre of the air, O swallow, swallow . . .
Myrrhina	. . . goddess of hope and light, guardian of vessels broken by the storm . . .
Phædra	. . . she wanders far . . .
Myrrhina	Not Delphi, not the isle Delos.

Myrrhina	. . . O white, white lily floating in the tide . . .
Phædra	. . . O queen, O bird, O star.
Choros	*We are the answer . . .*
Phædra	. . . luminous with phosphorescence . . .
Phædra	For the stark beauty of the name she bore . . .
Hyperides	. . . wan as a bride . . .
Hyperides	. . . and Phædra is your mother—
Hyperides	King, you are over-wrought and wild and see the wind howls ominously.

ACT III

Helios	. . . those who implore my guidance and my piloting at night . . . . . . and kept the sea silent with my enchantment . . .
Helios	. . . pilot and ships' guide . . .
Helios	. . . what high enchantment of the mountain shale . . .
Helios	O Delphian, guardian of sea-men . . . . . . ever present help, saviour and guardian . . .

Boy	. . . none pray him but he sends answer . . .
Boy	. . . and none go down into the avid sea but he accounts . . .
Boy	O loveliest—Athens' loveliest lost star—
Boy	His soul is beautiful in Love's great name—
Boy	His body blossoms as Adonis did—
Helios	You are less strong, O Delian, than love—
Hippolytus	. . . all the distant other-lands . . .
Artemis	O bright, O gold . . .
Helios	None, none is pure, and none, none is alone . . .
Artemis	How can I know if it be love or death?

ION

For B. Athens 1920
For P. Delphi 1932

Mr. Bernard Shaw, in his *Quintessence of Ibsenism,* writes of a
new element brought into modern drama by the Norwegian
school. "Ibsen was grim enough in all conscience; no man has
said more terrible things; and yet there is not one of Ibsen's
characters who is not, in the old phrase, the temple of the Holy
Ghost, and who does not move you at moments by the sense of
that mystery."Allowing for the great difference of treatment and
the comparative absence of detail in the ancient drama, this
phrase would, I think, be true of all the great Greek tragedians.
In Euripides it is clear enough.

—Gilbert Murray, *Euripides and His Age*

People of the Play

Hermes: the god
Ion: a young priest in the temple of Phoibos Apollo
Choros: the queen's waiting-women
Kreousa: queen of Athens
Xouthos: prince regent
An Old Man
A Servant
The Pythian Priestess
Athené: the goddess

Place: *Delphi*   Time: *Dawn*

TRANSLATOR'S NOTE

CLASSIC GREEK DRAMA *has no division and subdivision of act and scene. For convenience, the translator has divided this play into nineteen sections. These are preceded by explanatory notes. But these notes are merely the translator's personal interpretation; the play may be read straight through with no reference, whatever, to them.*

These nineteen divisions are sanctioned by the form of the play. Each one represents an entrance, an exit, a change in inner mood and external grouping of the characters. For any drama of the strictly classic or Periclean period, these are few in number. This play is fairly representative of the proportion; two gods who comment on the beginning and end; a messenger; in this case, a servant who is also an outside observer, half-way as it were, between the gods and men; a trinity of father, mother and son; the father, in this instance, being a divinity, has a double in the earthly manifestation of the king of Athens; an old man, a stock figure, and the Pythian priestess who, in the hands of this fifth-century "modern" genius, is freed from all taint of necromancy and seems also to predict a type made famous by Siena and Assisi; and last, and not least important, the choros.

The choros in a Greek play is, in a sense, a manifestation of its inner mood, expression, as it were, of group-consciousness; subconscious or superconscious comment on the whole. The strophe and antistrophe may be spoken by two separate members of the body of the ten or twelve, leaving the rest to interpret the words, in dance or pantomime, or merely to serve as formal background for the choros leader or leaders.

The translation is complete, with the exception of: the latter portion of Ion's monologue, Section VI; Section IX, the greater portion of the long, polemical discussion of Ion, in reply to the king, urging his return to Athens; a few lines in Ion's final speech in the same section; Antistrophe II, in Section XII; and the latter part of the Epilogue, which is historical narrative, having to do with a prophecy, concerning the future of the Ionian race.

It is significant that the word ION *has a double meaning. It may be translated by the Latin* UNUS, *meaning one, or first, and is also the Greek word for violet, the sacred flower of Athens.*

I

THE SYLLABLES *of these first lines are to be stressed like a gong. They must ring with a certain monotony and assurance. They are the call to attention, the announcement of a curtain about to rise. This curtain is purely imaginary. In fifth-century Greece, the speaker of the prologue enters direct. His entrance is more that of an orchestra-leader than an actor. He is, in fact, that. The quality and timbre of his voice are to set the rhythm of the whole performance.*

PROLOGUE

Hermes

The heaven is held aloft by a giant with
    arms of brass,
Atlas supports the house of the gods and
    the house-roof,
my mother's father; my mother is Maia,
    a goddess;
Hermes speaks, legate of the first of the
    gods, Zeus.

Roughly speaking, there were two types of theatre-goers in ancient Greece, as there are today. Those who are on time and those who are late. The prologue is the argument or libretto; it outlines the plot. The ardent lover of the drama will doubtless be strung up to a fine pitch of intensity and discrimination from the first. The presence of this actor, who impersonates the god Hermes, will actually be that god. Religion and art still go hand in hand. There is, in this country, as we all know, only one word to express its two most sacred abstractions, the good and the beautiful, to kalon.

We can imagine our enthusiast, as at an opening night of grand opera, being highly disorganized by the whispering of late comers, by the shuffling and readjustment of the audience. We can imagine our dilettante, our casual man-of-the-world, on the other hand, being highly annoyed to find that he has walked in, half-way through the tiresome, reiterated sing-song of the prologue. Then, as now, the character of a theatre-audience was of various degrees of literacy.

Enter the god.

He stands before us; already, we have taken his measure. He will or will not be able to cope with his difficult opening. He might bear a lighted torch. There is no conventional stage property for the speaker of this, or of any Attic prologue. But the torch is symbolical as well as practical. This is Delphi, still night, the sun has not yet risen.

There is no precedent, either, for his carrying a conventionally rolled script. But as writing is under the direct guardianship of this god, it might not be inappropriate. It would be effective if he could place the torch upright on a stand and read the bulky middle part of this prologue, almost chanting it. This would give a rhythmic, hypnotic effect and heighten mystery, in the manner of cathedral litany, heard at the far end of a great vault; our vault, here, is the dome of heaven. All later religious ritual, it might be remembered, is, in one way or another, derived through these earlier presentations. Greek drama was religious in intention, directly allied to the temple ceremonies. Our religious choirs and choruses are the direct descendant of this; a variation of this strophe and antistrophe has been familiar to most of us from childhood, though we may not remotely have guessed its antecedents.

This is Hermes. He has told us that. He is the god of writing, of writers, of orators, of the spoken word. Who could be more fitting as an introducer or announcer? He is the god of wit, of diplomacy, of games; the fleet-feet are, no doubt, bound with sandals. He speaks for his brother, master-musician and prophet, Helios, Phoibos, Apollo, Loxias, king of Delphi.

> I have come to Delphi:
> at the centre of earth:
> where Phoibos chants to men:
> priests interpret present and predict future
>   events:
> there is a town, noted throughout Hellas:
> named Athens, for Pallas of the gold-lance:
> there, Phoibos loved Kreousa:
> daughter of Erekhtheus, on the Acropolis:
> masters of Atthis call the place Makra:
> that Athenian cliff, great-rocks:
> the god kept her father ignorant:

she bore her secret, month by month:
in secret, she brought forth:
she took the infant to the grot:
her bride-chamber:
she left it, exposed as to death:
in the deep basket:
attribute of Erekhtheus, son of earth:
and his descendants:
along with the serpent-necklace:
gift to each true-born Athenian infant:
(because of Athené's first gift:
actual serpents to protect Erekhtheus:
whom daughters of Agraulos nursed):
so a Virgin decked her son for death:
but Helios, my brother, spoke:
go to the earth-born people of Athens:
you know the city of Pallas, you shall take:
out of a hollow rock, a new-born infant:
carry him, his garments and basket:
to Delphi, my prophetic seat:
set him before the entrance of my house:
as to the rest, I will see to it:
for I tell you alone:
this is my son:
I obeyed my brother, Loxias:
I found the reed-basket:
I left the child there, on these steps:
I opened the basket, revealed the contents:
dawn broke:
the prophetess came out:
she saw the child, started back:
what girl (she thought) has left:
a child of pleasure, on these steps:
she was about to cast it out:
but pity prevented that cruel act:
god watched, god wanted:
his child in his temple:

the pythoness brought him up:
she does not know Phoibos is his father:
nor who is his mother:
the boy knows no parents:
the altar gave him bread and life:
a child, he played about its steps:
now the Delphians vote him,
    temple-treasurer:
faithful steward, he is blameless in life:
Kreousa, his mother, married Xouthos:
the Khalkodonidae of Euboia made war on
    Athens:
Xouthos ended that fight:
though no Athenian, he was granted
    Kreousa, as tribute:
he is an Akhaian, son of Aiolos, son of
    Zeus:
long married, he and Kreousa are childless:
therefore they come to consult the Delphic
    oracle:
and Loxias arranges this.

It is necessary to stress the fact that the prologue is by way of being a programme. Or, if we are dealing in musical terms, it is the overture. All the threads of the story are indicated, the plot outlined, the leit-motif *sufficiently stressed. If we are passionate lovers of the drama, we may find this almost the most fascinating part of the play; on the other hand, many a budding Philhellene has struck a snag at the start, decided, on hasty perusal, that Greek drama is out of his depth and has let the whole thing go, after a single dreary attempt to follow the heavy and authoritative opening. Often, sententious platitudes are thrown out to mark time. We must get the audience settled, before we allow the leading actor or one of the almost equally important members of the small cast, to enter. This entrance must not be spoiled; the audience must be keyed-in to the theme, must be in receptive mood, must know roughly the trend of events, so that they may be sufficiently swayed but not over-excited, by certain of the later developments. Of nothing, too much.*

The original speech of the prologue is declaimed without a break. The translator has arranged it in three sections, however, to bring it a little nearer the level of present-day convention.

At Delphi, the enormous stars are still shining. Our prologue stands with his back to the great pillars of the famous temple. The tiers of steps, behind him, seem to mount to infinity. The eyes of the fleet-foot legate of God face us, they face the mountains, above which, a faint glow announces the coming of day. Yet still, the great stars burn in darkness, and still, we ask ourselves what can this all signify; is this a worthy theme for great religious drama, the betrayal and desertion, by one of its most luminous figures, of a woman and her first child? but before the thought actually has time to crystallize, the silver rhythms of this subtle defendant, God's messenger, silence us.

Not meaningless, as you might think,
are the god's plans,
he will give his son to a king,
who will enter this gate,
he will say to Xouthos,
this child is a child of your youth,
so that the boy may go back,
to his mother's house;
his mother shall know him
but the god's act be hid;
the child shall be happy:

not meaningless, as you might think,
are the god's plans,
Asia shall share his fame
and the eastern lands
boast, when they say,
we are called by that name,
Ionians;
this is his wish,
and thus the god speaks,
my son shall be called Ion,
by the men of Greece:

not meaningless, as you might think,
but the time comes
for me to enter the temple,
to hear within,
prophecies of the future;
I turn toward the laurel-gate;
but see—he comes—the son of the god
draws near,
bearing a laurel-branch
to hang on the portal:
now of the gods,
I am first of the gods to speak
a name, famous hereafter,
among men, among gods, among Greeks

ION

II

THE SUN RISES *at Delphi.*

*To the acute mind of the fifth-century Hellene this is no miracle.
Yet this is the miracle. At this moment, in the heart-beat of world-
progress, in the mind of every well-informed Greek—and who of that
shifty, analytical, self-critical, experimental race of the city of Athens, at
any rate, was not well-informed?—there was a pause (psychic, intellectual), such a phase as we are today experiencing; scientific discovery
had just opened up world-vistas, at the same time the very zeal of practical
knowledge, geometry, astronomy, geography, was forcing the high-
strung intellect on a beat further beyond the intellect. As today, when
time values and numerical values are shifting, due to the very excess of
our logical deductions, so here. A great English critic has used this play to
point out forcibly the irony and rationalism in the mind of the poet. We do
not, however, altogether accept his estimates.*

*Is Euripides ironical, or has his knife-edge mind seen round the
edge, round the corner, as the greatest scientists and thinkers of today are
doing? Has the circle turned, the serpent again bitten its own tail? This
Greek knew that the sun would rise. Yet he hails its coming, as a miracle.*

*As a student, a thinker, a philosopher, an Athenian, a Greek (only
just—at sixty—freed from military service, hence one of the "gerontes"),
does this "old man" throw his psyche back into the first lyrical intensities
of youth? In spite of the so-called rationalists, and the much-quoted critic
with his "irony is lurking at every corner," I prefer to believe that the poet
speaks through his boy-priest, Ion, with his own vibrant superabundance
of ecstasy before a miracle; the sun rises.*

Ion
    O, my Lord,
    O, my king of the chariot,
    O, four-steeds,
    O, bright wheel,
    O, fair crest
    of Parnassus you just touch:
    (O, frail stars,
    fall,
    fall back from his luminous onslaught:)

O, my Lord,
O, my king,
O, bright Helios,
god of fire,
from your altar,
more fire drifts
and smoke
from the incense of sweet-myrrh;

O, my Lord,
from your tripod
the sounds ring,
of the Pythoness
chanting to all Greece,
your commands,
so we greet you,
so we sing;

you are fair,
you are fire,
you are Helios.

Enter priests, from the temple.

You are fair,
you are Delphian
high-priests;
your lips
tuned to his lips,
will soon speak
clear words
to interpret
the magic
oracular
Voice
from the altar;
you will answer
the men here,
who worship;

they are fair;
these high-priests
seek Kastalia,
they will bathe
in that silver, swift
river.

We may relegate the boy, Ion, to the dust-heap and parse his delicate phrases till we end in a mad-house. It will bring us no nearer to the core of Greek beauty. Parse the sun in heaven, distinguish between the taste of mountain air on different levels, feel with your bare foot a rock covered with sea-weed, one covered with sand, one washed and marbled by the tide. You can not learn Greek, only, with a dictionary. You can learn it with your hands and your feet and especially with your lungs.

Taste snow in the air, and distinguish the different qualities and intensities of the wind as it rises from the deep gorge before this temple, or from the drop off the cliffs to the sea, behind it. Realize with some sixth sense, the sea; know that it is there, by the special quality of the shimmering of bay-leaf or some hinted reflex from the sky-dome. Extract from this strophe, one fact; the water is cold in the little river that cuts in a rocky gash, through the other hollow, opposite the temple's sea-side. Does Ion envy these young priests this early-morning, ritualistic libation? We judge so.

Here,
I have other work,
I bind
the sacred wreaths;
I sweep the holy gate,
and with my laurel-branch,
the steps
before the house;
I lave
the marble pavement;
with bow and dart,
I chase
birds

who would mar the gifts;
this was my home
from birth;
this always
was my life;
fatherless,
motherless,
I praise
this sacred place,
the temple
and the god,
Helios.

Gesture may be simple, direct copy of marble arm and bared limb of pentellic frieze, or it may tune-in to a less formal era, romantic beat and barbaric rhythm that have become familiar through the exotic present-day ballet. There is nothing that cannot be done, choreographically, with these few stanzas. Ion has a choice of decorative properties; the golden bow, tall jars or flat bowls and water-pots, the flat gilded wreath or wreaths bound in the rough, bright natural-green boughs or branches, ready for trimming and decoration. Ion may even cut and trim these as he speaks; he moves about with his broom or switch of bound myrtle-twigs. He may stand, in hieratic posture, scarcely moving, uttering frigid remote syllables like a marble statue, or he has the whole run and rhythm of near-eastern colour and exoticism to draw on. He raises his laurel-branch, as a water-diviner, his rod.

Strophe   Laurel,
most beautiful,
O, bright
laurel
that sweeps the steps
and the court
of the god Helios;
laurel
gathered within
an immortal laurel-garden,

laurel
cut from a stream
that creeps from a myrtle-thicket
(O, haunted water and blest),
O, laurel,
O, myrtle,
I break
your branch
as the day breaks;
each day
as that avid wing
sweeps blindingly upward,
I bring
fresh laurel
to deck this place;

O, laurel,
O, myrtle,
O, Paian;
O, Paian,
O, laurel,
O, Leto's son;

Antistrophe

let me praise
this spirit,
this home;
let me revere
altar, pillar, rare
tasks I have done;
work can not tire
priests, servants;
immortal joy waits
immortal devotes;

branch sweep
no more,
water-jar
now pour

water,
and gold ewer,
come give
river-water,
hands spray
pure silver,
Kastalia's
crystal water,
lips praise and pray
our father,
no mortal;

O, laurel,
O, myrtle,
O, Paian;
O, Paian,
O, laurel,
O, Leto's son;

Birds flock in here from the high air, above Parnassus. That mountain still towers, unassailable, as in our imagination, the actual temple of the god, though actually its old body, its dead shell lies a heap of battered rocks, its holy-of-holies open to rain and ruin. Long after the actual dæmon was canonically ejected from his immemorial home, a Presence still haunted those weathered stones and spiritually impermeated rocks. So intense and vivid was its power, that those fanatic monks who spared the temple of that sister power, the Virgin of Athens, frantically tore with their own hands at stones, imbued with a Weltgeist *of such inner potency, that its magic threatened even their sincerity. So mighty was the inviolable spirit of this place that those monks, with their utmost fervour, could only dislodge a small number of its blocks, could only break off a small proportion of the images of its façade and of its memorial figures, at turnings of the paved sacred way. So mighty was the reputation of Delphi, that the later apostate, in his dream of a spiritual Greek renaissance, sent ambassadors, in their costliest apparel, with pack animals laden with curious treasures, to hint (subtle bribery) to the meagre body of attendant priests that their day was not yet over. His emissaries, or the Byzantine monarch himself, posed the famous question, "shall the old gods return?" So incontrovertible was its two-edged honour that, even in those days of its imminent decline, that meagre handful of doomed priests preferred Delphic integrity to offers of fantastic power and wealth, and sent back to the emperor Julian at Constantinople, the last message of their oracle, "the new God has risen; the oracle is silent; He has conquered; the water-spring is dried up; the laurel is withered." So powerful, still, was the innate mystery of those forsaken halls, those corridors, that paved sacred way, those altars, that only God himself could break it. A final earthquake sent those mighty walls hurtling down hill, the façade to lie among thistles, the gold to be fouled and tarnished by lizard, snail and the serpent, until brigands finally pried out all the gold that was left, and wandering shepherds, gathering what stone seemed suitable for their mountain huts, left those more fearful broken, marble bits of hands and feet, cursed by man and God alike, to crumble in frost and sun. So incontrovertible is the power of beauty, that within the last century, men of almost superhuman intuition, intellectual devotion and integrity, archæologists of France, have managed to trace wide scattered fragments and re-build, almost in its entirety, the ancient treasure-house of the Athenians at Delphi. Now sharp Ionic columns start up, shafts of unblemished marble point the way to a return; worship the eternal. Indestructible beauty lives.*

So this manuscript of the poet, Euripides, was spared when so much perished; no Savonarola of antiquity or the Middle Ages had power against it. The eagle soars today above the crags of Parnassus. The boy Ion speaks.

Ion	Bird
	of the air,
	O, bright legate,
	wing back,
	back,
	I say,
	to Parnassus;
	off, off the cornice,
	that bright peak,
	that gold ledge
	is no perch for your feet;

O, eagle,
back,
back,
where you hold court,
commanding all birds
with your sharp beak;
back, back to your nest
on Parnassus;

bird
of the lake,
O, fair,
fairest
of birds
and beloved of king Phoibos,
O, swan
of the white wing,
the red feet,
wing back,
back, I say,
to lake Delos;
O, voice that is tuned
to his harp-note,
O, throat
must I pierce you
with my dart?
be off,
O, my swan
lest your blood drip
red death
on this beautiful pavement;

bird
of the wood,
must you have gold?
these gifts
were not set here

for bird-nests;
bird,
bird
of the woods,
seek your forests
by the isthmus
or near
river Alpheus,
my dart
warns you,
here it is dangerous
for you
and your fledgelings;
O, be off;
my arrow has no choice,
nor I;
I am the god's
and I obey;

but
O, you birds
of lake and forest,
you swan,
you wood-bird
and you legate
of Zeus,
even as I string my bow,
I pray,
be off,
be off,
for I must slay
intruders here
within the precinct;

back to Parnassus
and your nests,
back,
back,

O, God's majestic legate,
back,
back,
O, swan,
my Lord's delight,
back,
back,
O, little birds who sing;

for this,
O, this, I would not kill,
your song
that tells to men,
God's will.

III

THE CHOROS is, as it were, an outside voice, punctuating and stressing moods. It is the play's collective conscience. However, from time to time, speakers of strophe or antistrophe merge, informally, with the actors, or serve to bind contrasting moods. We may imagine that the ladies-in-waiting who enter here, stroll informally, as they might have done in their own city, Athens, through the corridors of this famous temple.

Personally, I visualize them in blue, one colour of various shades. The strict continuity may be indicated by veils of one shape, but from time to time, as in this instance, it seems to me, the individuality of the members might be stressed. They stand against columns of a temple that may or may not be painted. That stone grandeur was also intensified by primitive bands or upright stripes; black, vermilion, azure, crocus tones are now lost, but they would roughly approximate the effects that the sands and heat of Egypt have baked in, there, for eternity. Certainly, dazzling white features here, as never in Egypt. We may choose our mood, however.

These visitors are intensely interested in the temple. It will be remembered that, in Athens, the Parthenon, on the site of the old shrine but lately destroyed by the Persians, has actually been in a state of construction. Here, we may imagine frescoes painted, in the manner of early Italian primitives. The poet, a painter in youth, is no doubt actually describing art treasures of Delphi itself.

1st semi-choros	O, Athens,
Strophe I	Athens,
	we revere
	your god-of-the-beautiful-street;
	O, Athens,
	we know how fair
	are your altars,
	how white
	your pillars,
	but no more fair
	than this
	twin-pediment

that reflects the light
of Helios,
child of Leto;

2nd semi-choros   O, Athens,
we know that you are fair,
but here,
what grace,
look where the son of Zeus
strikes at the Lernian pest,
look at this gold,
his knife;

1st semi-choros   Look at this torch; how fair,
Antistrophe I   this cuirass;
is it Iolaos
who helped the son of Zeus?
once,
I embroidered this;

2nd semi-choros   look at this horse
who leaps
upwards with wings,
with this
hero
who slays a beast,
three bodied,
with fiery breath—

1st semi-choros   —and
Strophe II   this—

2nd semi-choros   look at that wall of granite,
the fight of the giants—

1st semi-choros   —here,
there—

2nd semi-choros	—and this who holds aloft the aegis, dragon-wrought, threatening Enkelados; who is it?
1st semi-choros	Pallas, goddess—
2nd semi-choros	—and here fire shoots from the great hand of Zeus—
1st semi-choros	—yes, yes, he kills a giant, Mimas, the hideous; and with his ivy-staff (ivy is meant for peace), Bromios slays a son of earth.

Their delight before the carved and painted treasures of the temple repeat, in minor tone, the rapt intensity of the words of the boy, Ion, who during or before this scene has crept off, perhaps to a distant point of vantage, to stalk another of these foragers, those birds whom he so loves and whom, contradictorily, he must slay. The women see him now. Perhaps they have come across him, in a far corner where they have clustered to examine the last fresco or painting or sculptured group. Or else the boy himself has walked toward them, realizing no casual visitors, but people of importance, whose head-dresses and embroidered robes proclaim them inmates of some great house. He waits without speaking, until one of the women addresses him.

Choros *Antistrophe II*	Hail, you before the temple-gate, we wish to enter, may we pass?
Ion	you may not;
Choros	may we ask a question?
Ion	ask;
Choros	does actually, this inner court guard omphalos, earth's sacred rock?
Ion	yes; garlands deck the sacred place, where Gorgons watch;
Choros	ah, famous spot;
Ion	if you would enter to consult the oracle, you must first make propitiation, special gift of a slain ewe;
Choros	we only want to look about; we would not violate these rites;
Ion	look where you will;

Choros	our lords invited us to visit here;
Ion	what lords? from where?
Choros	Athenian rulers; ah, but there, our lady comes, go, ask of her.

IV

THE QUEEN OF ATHENS *stands before us. How long has she been standing? If the delicate robes of her waiting-women are kingfisher or midnight blue, hers seem to fall in folds that are cut of pure stone, lapis. She has always been standing there. She seems, simply, a temple property that we have, so far, neglected. Her women move, singly or in groups, through the corridors, taking, for all their elegant convention, humanity with them. Kreousa has the inhumanity of a meteor, sunk under the sea.*

The boy knows this.

He recognizes it.

Here is something akin to himself; here is rock, air, wings, loneliness. Who is this?

We do not know how long they stand, looking at one another.

The boy at least, is staring at his mother. He realizes, however, with a start, that her eyes are closed. Apparently, she has been standing rapt, gazing at the holy beauty of the temple. But this is not so. Her eyes are fast shut.

Ion	O, beautiful woman,
	who are you?
	O, rare beauty,
	O, grace that proclaims you
	a princess,
	O, goddess,
	what rain
	mars that marble,
	your face?
	eyes shut
	in a mask,
	see not glory,
	nor beauty,
	nor this place;
	you weep,
	while others all rejoice
	in this splendour,
	the temple
	of Loxias.

Kreousa   O, fair,
O, strange voice,
it is right
that you ask
why I weep;
I looked on this house,
I was caught
by an ancient regret;
I stood here,
I was far off,
I thought:
"you are doomed,
race of women,
O, woman
and women,
and lost;
why hope
and of whom can you hope,
whom the Dæmons
betray—"

Ion   speak not,
O, what torment—

Kreousa   my arrow is gone;
who let fly
venomed anger,
is quiet.

A woman is about to step out of stone, in the manner of a later Rodin. It is impossible, at this moment, not to swing forward into a—to fifth-century Greece—distant future. This poetry rises clean cut today, as it did at the time of its writing. And today, we may again wonder at this method and manner of portraiture, for the abstract welded with human implication, is in its way, ultra-modern.

A woman is about to break out of an abstraction and the effect is terrible. We wish she would go back to our preconceived ideas of what classic characterization should be. It seems this queen of Athens had leapt

forward that odd 450 years that separates this classic age from our own.
She is mother of sorrows, indeed.

Ion   who are you?
who are you?
what city?
what name?

Kreousa   Kreousa,
an Erekhthian,
of Athens.

Ion   O, dweller in a famous place,
what parents,
what city,
what race;
I envy,
O, I envy you this—

Kreousa   envy this,
but naught else—

Ion   is it true,
what men say?

Kreousa   is what true?
I would know—

Ion   earth begot,
your begettor?

Kreousa   Erekhtheus, yes;
can race help?

Ion   freed from earth
by Athené?

Kreousa   by her hands,
virgin, motherless.

If we knew Greek perfectly and had each one of us the peculiar gift of rhythmic sensitiveness and awareness of tone value of skilled musicians, we might manage to convey in the spoken words something of the emotional tension behind them. Or on the other hand, if we were completely conventionalized mummers in masks, speaking by rote, in a sort of hypnotic sing-song, we might deal with this dialogue in a convincing manner. Or else, if we were standing before an altar, really deeply moved, part of an immense ritualistic ceremony, attuned to audience and the god beyond the altar, we might arrive at some satisfactory emotional solution. What is there left for us?

The broken, exclamatory or evocative vers-libre *which I have chosen to translate the two-line dialogue, throughout the play, is the exact antithesis of the original. Though concentrating and translating sometimes, ten words, with two, I have endeavoured, in no way, to depart from the meaning. The son and mother outline this same story in suave metres. Their manner is that of skilled weavers, throwing and returning the shuttle of contrasting threads. There are just under a hundred of these perfectly matched statements, questions and answers. The original reads as sustained narrative.*

The choros returns towards the end of this dialogue.

Ion	—yes, in pictures—
Kreousa	—Kekrop's daughters—
Ion	—had a basket—
Kreousa	—but their neglect—
Ion	—caused their own death—
Kreousa	—Erekhtheus—
Ion	—from the great cliff—
Kreousa	—hurled the sisters—
Ion	—how were you left?

Kreousa	—still an infant—
Ion	then an earthquake—
Kreousa	—blow of trident—
Ion	—slew your father?
Kreousa	O, rock Makra—
Ion	—Pythia claims it—
Kreousa	—evil, evil—
Ion	—dare you say it?
Kreousa	—crime was done there—
Ion	—whose wife are you?
Kreousa	—of a stranger—
Ion	—but a great prince?
Kreousa	—grand-son of Zeus—
Ion	—strange to your rocks?
Kreousa	—near Euboia—
Ion	—sea-waves wash it—
Kreousa	—Xouthos helped us—
Ion	—his sword won you?
Kreousa	—prize of combat—

Ion   —are you alone?

Kreousa   —with my husband—

Ion   —what do you want?

Kreousa   —we ask one thing—

Ion   —wealth or children?

Kreousa   —we are childless—

Ion   —you are childless?

Kreousa   —Phoibos knows it—

Ion   O, my poor heart—

Kreousa   —you, who are you?

Ion   —the god's servant—

Kreousa   —given or sold here?

Ion   I am Loxias'—

Kreousa   —child, your mother?

Ion   I don't know her—

Kreousa   —where is your house?

Ion   —this is my house—

Kreousa   —you have been here—

Ion   —ever since birth—

Kreousa	—who was your nurse?
Ion	I knew no nurse.
Kreousa	O, I weep now—
Ion	Pythia loved me—
Kreousa	—but since grown up?
Ion	—strangers help me—
Kreousa	—but your mother?
Ion	I am, maybe—
Kreousa	—no; what fine stuff—
Ion	—robe of a priest—
Kreousa	—but your parents?
Ion	I have no clue—
Kreousa	—ah, the same hurt—
Ion	—what hurt—tell me—
Kreousa	—I have come here—
Ion	—you have come here?
Kreousa	—for a friend's sake—
Ion	—what does she want?
Kreousa	—I dare not speak—

Ion	—speak and tell me—
Kreousa	—she was Phoibos'—
Ion	—do not say that—
Kreousa	—and had his child—
Ion	—no, a man's act—
Kreousa	—no—it was god—
Ion	—child of Phoibos?
Kreousa	—hid in the rocks—
Ion	—where—where is it?
Kreousa	—she bids me ask—
Ion	—has it perished?
Kreousa	—she thinks, wild beasts—
Ion	—but why think that?
Kreousa	—she looked for it—
Ion	—did she find tracks?
Kreousa	—there was no trace—
Ion	—when was all this?
Kreousa	—how old are you?
Ion	—could god do that?

Kreousa	—her first—her last—
Ion	Phoibos took it?
Kreousa	—if so—alas—
Ion	—is there no hope?
Kreousa	—for you—what hope?
Ion	—for me? don't speak—
Kreousa	—poor child—she asks
Ion	—but one weak point—
Kreousa	—one? all is black—

Ion
will god speak of that
which he would keep hidden?
alas, how dare we ask?

Kreousa
the tripod is given by god
to the whole of Greece,
to answer, what we ask;

Ion
how dare we question the god
and injure his honour?

Kreousa
and of her, of whom we speak,
whom he made suffer?

Ion
Are you mad?
what priest
dare invoke
in his house,
a voice,

to speak judgment
on him,
whom the augurers
worship?
have you lost
all sense of yourself?
do you think
we may challenge the god,
and here, in his very-house?
how barren,
how profitless,
were prophecy,
forced
by the high-priest;
what good were it
to consult
bird-flight
or the slain beast
for auguries,
which the god
forbids?
provoke not
unwilling utterance;
it were useless
and worse than useless;

Choros

many
are the griefs of man,
many,
many,
each different;
many are the sorrows
and strange,
of man,
the unfortunate;

Kreousa

so,
here and in that other place,
you are equally negligent,

so,
holy Phoibos,
you never saved that poor child,
who was yours to protect,
nor now
reply to that woman
(whom,
absent,
I represent),
so that she may seek the tomb,
at least, know
he is no more here,
but a shadow;
so,
holy Phoibos,
why ask further
(for her whom you disown),
of you,
who are god?

but
speak not
of this;
they are back
from the grot
of Trophonius;
Xouthos
would misinterpret
the act of this woman;

O, poor
lost woman
and race of women,
alike;
O, chaste,
O, lawless;
man made your law;
for you all,
there is one
judgment.

IN HIS OWN WAY, *this chieftain from a neighbouring province of Greece is a no less impressive person than the queen herself. Probably, in a purely mundane sense, he is more striking. This king may appear alone, from this subsidiary visit to the preliminary oracle, the grot or altar of Trophonius, or accompanied, for the sake of effect, with any number of soldiers, a group of civil attendants or young aristocrats. It may be imagined that he would wear sumptuous garments for this state visit to the oracle. He is inquiring not only for himself, but, as it were, for the whole of Hellas, concerning its future ruler, his heir.*

In the last section, there was a tense feeling of ecstasy and an undercurrent of hysteria, as if the pent emotions of a childless woman and of a motherless boy might, at any moment, break through the surface of hard-won reticence. Here is a counter to all that. The queen's unconscious hatred may stab out at her husband, in vituperative innuendo, nevertheless he stands there, solid, conservative, loyal. He does not even faintly realize her predicament; that is fortunate. If Xouthos had met her, had touched, at all, on her other life, she would not have been able to keep this inner sacred chamber of her spirit, free. She has lived only half a life with him. No doubt, he has guessed this, but his queen will never know it.

Fate has given him a difficult part to play. He plays it with dignity and without imagination.

Xouthos	Hail,
	O, Phoibos;
	may the god
	be honoured first;
	next,
	hail,
	O my queen;
	Am I late?
	you are frightened?
Kreousa	no,
	no;
	only

waiting—
anxious—
tell me
what the oracle says;
do we remain
hopeless?

Xouthos   Trophonius
does not predict,
but says,
"wait the god's utterance;"
nevertheless,
he too spoke;
neither you nor I
shall return
childless.

Kreousa   O,
holiest mother,
perhaps, after all,
our visit
was fortunate,
perhaps, after all,
your son
may be fair
to us;

Xouthos   fair?
but, of course;
where is the god's
prophet?

Ion   I watch
the outer court,
beyond,
nobles of Delphi,
chosen by lot,
guard
the innermost temple;

Xouthos	my thanks;
	I am ready
	to enter;
	I hear,
	in fact,
	that the oracle
	now speaks
	within the court,
	for all worshippers;
	let this holy-day
	be propitious;
	take
	laurel-branches
	and wait,
	O, queen,
	by the altar;
	ask there,
	that I return from the inner house,
	with good news
	of the future;
Kreousa	ask?
(aside)	ask?
	take laurel?
	he has yet a chance,
	this One,
	to repair hurt;
	ask?
	ask?
	he may yet grant
	help;
	in any case,
	I am powerless;
	I cannot accept
	the Dæmon,
	but I accept
	the Voice.

VI

Aʟʟ ᴛʜɪꜱ ᴛɪᴍᴇ *our Greek sky has been changing.*

Ion carries the laurel-branch, attribute of priesthood, the wand of power. This branch has been, so far, only the humble instrument of a boy-sweep before a temple. Nevertheless, we can imagine gestures that might well command the whole circle of the hours. What time is it?

Greek unity gives us freedom, it expands and contracts at will, it is time-in-time and time-out-of-time together, it predicts modern time-estimates. But the sun, at any rate, has been rising.

It must be very hot, or there is an expectation of heat, a feeling toward propitiation, as the boy turns to the water-jars, in order, not only to cleanse, but to cool the great square stones that lie flat to the blaze of the Lord of heaven, before the threshold of his very house.

Ion
    Why does she talk like this,
    this woman?
    what does she hint?
    she seems to hide something;
    she speaks
    cryptically;
    would she consult
    the Voice
    for herself
    or another?
    in either case,
    she blames Helios;
    but what does it matter?
    Erekhtheus's daughter
    means nothing
    to me;
    Erekhtheus?
    daughter?
    who are these people?
    I'll get on with my work,
    sprinkling water
    from this vase

or this gold jar;
but—

Helios,
answer me;
say
you are blameless;
could you take
a mere child
and betray her?
could you betray her
and leave
your own child
to die?
no,
no,
no,
you are our Lord,
our virtue—

you punish
man's evil;
you could not
(it were unjust),
break laws
made for mortals.

VII

THOUGH THE FUNCTION *of the choros is primarily spiritual, or in a subtle poetical sense, psychological, it has also its very definite useful purpose. Not the least of its utilitarian functions is that of serving for what modern drama means, in its full sense, when it alludes, in one way or another, to the, or to a "curtain." The falling of a curtain, in present-day dramatic art, as we all know, does not simply mean that the room or outdoor scene is shut off. Time is marked, and in subtle ways; even the shortest time indicated may be pregnant with other-idea, other mood or other dramatic pattern. So too, with these women, when they sing or chant or recite words. The words often are complete and logical comment, on the play's progress. Yet sometimes they have no more to do with it than the decorative sign of (say) a historical pageant dropped across an indoor "period" scene to which it has no actual relation in time or space. To the fifth-century Athenian, much of the mythological ornament of the choros is purely decorative.*

On the other hand, this poet had, we have been told, a disconcerting way of shocking the sensibilities of his contemporaries. This antistrophe, for instance, is curiously "human," startlingly personal, after the sonorous appeal of the strophe to chriselephantine beauty and flawless, detached, deified virginity.

Strophe

You who have never known
the perils of birth,
you who were born,
with the help of a giant,
Prometheus,
from the forehead
of Zeus,
come,
O, Athené,
come;
step down
from the marble wall,
from the gold shale
of Olympos;

come
to the earth-heart,
the tripod,
the temple
of Phoibos;
chant,
O, great Niké,
and you,
Artemis,
sister of Helios,
Virgins both,
pray to the Voice,
pray to the tripod,
the dance;
lest Erekhtheus' race be lost,
grant a child,
O, child
of Leto:

Antistrophe

for what is a man's life
without children?
his court
is flowerless;
his wealth
is a barren gain,
without a child
to enjoy it;
what is a child?
a help
in sorrow;
a joy
in peace;
in war,
our very-heart,
the throb of our heart-beat;
O, give me a child
for delight,

no royal palace;
O, childless,
O, barren wife,
how dead your heart
if you think,
luxury better than this,
a child's touch,
a child's kiss.

Epode   O,
grot
of Pan
and rock
close to the rock of Makra,
you saw three sisters dance;
grass swayed
by the porch of Pallas;
the rocks gave back the notes
of your flute,
O, Pan,
in that place,
where a Virgin
left a child,
her child
and the child of Phoibos;
O, unhappy girl,
she left
her child,
prey of the wild-hawks;

O, tell me,
have you seen,
woven on tapestries,
a happy tale of a child,
born of god and a woman?
have you heard such a tale spoken?

VIII

Stage directions *for a Greek play must be entirely inferred from the context. We do not know whether the boy has been standing the whole time, sitting thoughtfully on the steps, wandering about with his myrtle-branch or erect in some rapt pose, as he watches the distant sky for the down-flight of some hovering bird, or whether he walked away with the last tragic questioning about the purpose of his divinity. Did he go into the temple to gain spiritual strength? Has he been listening to the choirs inside, the harpists, the lute and flute-players? Has he stood outside the very sacred circle that surrounds the holy-of-holies, the tripod where the high-priestess, the Pythia, gives the strange two-edged answers to those who have come to learn the future, at this famous shrine? Does he himself ponder the wording of a question, which, later, he is on the point of asking: who he is, after all, and how he had got here?*

We can only infer something of all this, let our own imaginations fill out this harmonious outline. We can, if we are strictly of a purist tendency, leave the place bare, imagine the choros in hieratic posture, scarcely moving. Or we can imagine the trail of various priests, officials from the town even, visitors who may cross and re-cross, votaries with presents. The mind has full power of expanding the "romantic" life, in and out of the court, the come and go of worshippers through the great doors. Or, as I say, we may preserve the strictly "classic" outline, the great pillars, the formal tense figures of the chanting women.

Ion	Hail, you before the temple gate, O, women, answer; where is your master?
	and what does the tripod sing? what hope has your king?

Choros   we know not,
               he waits within
               but there—

               the sound of the bolts,
               they throw back
               the temple-door,

               he is here.

IX

IF ONE DEPARTS *from strict ritual, entrance, exit, the upraised palms of prayer, the mystic circle of dance, the stately entrance, at most, of a few priests in the background, one's imagination takes one, perhaps, too far. How far? Music seems to break across, a clash as of muffled cymbals from within the temple, as the great doors swing back and the king, a god-like figure, straight from the inner sanctuary, with the light of a god and the message on his face, steps forth.*

Enter Xouthos. There is no stage-direction necessary, all that is indicated by the words of the poet: "he is here," says the choros of waiting women, but what does that signify? It may be simply a conventional remark, made in answer to a conventional question. It may be an exclamation, as the king, born of a son of a son of Zeus, stands in royal robes, his most beautiful ornaments, but lately put on to honour this god, this king of prophecy and music, Apollo. The light of music, song, rejoicing shines from his face. For the moment, he is transformed by joy, into the likeness of the sun-god, not the youth with bow and arrow or the young musician with the strung harp, but an older, mystical son of the King of Heaven: they are after all distantly related, this boy and this man, whose claims for fatherhood are so quickly doubted.

Does Xouthos walk slowly down the great steps? Does he stand and look at the boy, for a long time, before he speaks, or does his voice resound instantly, like a trumpet, from the door-way?

Xouthos	My own—my beloved—
Ion	—own? beloved?
Xouthos	—your hand—your face—
Ion	—madness—
Xouthos	O, I would only touch—
Ion	—not this—the priest's head-dress—

Xouthos	I find you—
Ion	—and this arrow—
Xouthos	—and you, me—
Ion	—my quiver—my bow—
Xouthos	—you attack your own father—
Ion	—never—father—
Xouthos	—it's true—
Ion	—how?
Xouthos	—we are father and son—
Ion	—who says so?
Xouthos	—the god, your protector—
Ion	—with you, the one witness—
Xouthos	I quote the god's utterance—
Ion	—you mis-read a riddle—
Xouthos	—did I misinterpret?
Ion	—what was his exact speech?
Xouthos	—the first one that I met—
Ion	—you met—where?
Xouthos	—coming out of the temple—

Ion	—yes—should be—
Xouthos	—my son—
Ion	—your own or adopted?
Xouthos	—adopted, but my own—
Ion	—I was first?
Xouthos	—no one else—
Ion	O, strange fate—
Xouthos	—for me, strange—
Ion	—yet—my mother?
Xouthos	I don't know her—
Ion	—does the god know?
Xouthos	I did not ask—
Ion	—am I earth-born?
Xouthos	—earth-born?
Ion	—how am I your son?
Xouthos	—the god said so—
Ion	O—no more—
Xouthos	—my child, as you wish—
Ion	—yet—some affair—

Xouthos	—youth—youth—
Ion	—before you wed?
Xouthos	—never since—
Ion	—and *that's* my nobility—
Xouthos	—your age is about right—
Ion	—how did I get here?
Xouthos	I don't know—
Ion	—from far or near?
Xouthos	I can't say—
Ion	—had you ever stayed here?
Xouthos	—for the mysteries of Bakkhos—
Ion	—alone?
Xouthos	—with a partner—
Ion	—where? whom? what?
Xouthos	—with a Mainad—
Ion	—and you?
Xouthos	—had drunk of the wine-cup—
Ion	—so—
Xouthos	—child, it is fate—

Ion	—but how did I get here?
Xouthos	—perhaps left by that girl—
Ion	—escaped—for this—
Xouthos	O, speak to your father—
Ion	—it is the god's wish—
Xouthos	—at last, you are wise—
Ion	—what more could I ask?
Xouthos	—you do see, at last—
Ion	—a descendant of Zeus—
Xouthos	—it is fate—fate—
Ion	—hail; you gave me life—
Xouthos	—you obey god—
Ion	—my father—
Xouthos	—ah, sweet word—
Ion	—well met—
Xouthos	I am happy.
Ion	But O, my mother, whoever you are, will I never see your face? I want that more than ever;

are you dead,
mother?

Choros   I felicitate
this house,
nevertheless,
I could wish
that the queen
were not childless,
and the race
of Erekhtheus.

Xouthos   O, my child,
the god
has directed things
on your behalf;
we have met;
your natural desire
is mine,
to find your mother;
there is time for that;
leave this place,
come with me,
you shall share
my sceptre
in Athens;
do not fear,
you are rich,
of noble blood;
you are silent?
why do you look
like this?
your face turns
from joy
to despair;

Ion   things seen far off

and near,
are different;
indeed, I felicitate fate
since I have found you,
father;
but listen;
I think
the Athenians,
that earth-born race,
will hate me,
an outsider,
illegitimate,
how fight against it?
if I attain prominence,
I shall be despised;
I shall be despised,
if I do not;

Choros

well said;
may you bring happiness
to her
whom we love most:

Xouthos

but enough
of worry and talk;
can't you be happy?
the moment
I heard of this,
I commanded
a banquet set
in a festive place,
for a guest;
O, I would celebrate
a birth-day,
my son's,
at last;
O, guest of honour,

rejoice,
you return
to your father's house.

Ion   I come;
           but, father,
           forgive me
           and my soul
           that asks:

           where is she,
           that woman,
           my mother?

X

AGAIN *the choros. This time, no decorative expression, pattern of mood simply to mark time, or rhythmic merging of one value with another. They breathe bitter and fiery words as if to prophesy the unconscious reaction of their queen. They feel as one, as a proud, deserted woman might feel.*

Having, as it were, expressed the inner fire and concentrated bitterness of the queen, they perform again their function of "curtain." They indicate time passed and a not inconsiderable space of time, by the fact that the boy and his father are well advanced on the long and difficult journey up toward the heights of Parnassus.

The few words of the epode inflame our imagination. We see a mighty procession, sacrificers, other priestly attendants, a whole company of servants, carpenters, musicians, wine-servants, and last and not least, the delicately stepping donkeys with flagons wrapped in vine-leaves and the bulky jars strung aside their backs. Other animals, too, the asses, goats, the sacrificial rams or bulls, strung, unquestionably, with coloured wool fillets and decorative garlands.

Choros	Tears, tears
Strophe	wild grief,
	pity,
	pity my mistress;
	O, what will our lady
	think,
	when she sees her husband
	and asks,
	"who is this,
	this beautiful youth?
	what is it
	the prophet grants?
	a child to his house;
	I am left
	deserted
	and childless;"

who is this child?
who left
this waif
on the temple-steps?
O, oracle,
you are dark,
you are hiding
a mystery,
there is danger lurking,
a trap;
these are not happy portents;
do you feel it?
this child is cursed:

Antistrophe   shall we speak?
shall we tell her this?
she gave her entire life
to this man who betrays
her trust;
old age
will find her hopeless,
while he will have joy;
in his heart,
he will hate her;
her loneliness
will remind him
of how he stole,
nameless,
into her house
to usurp
her noble name;
O death,
death strike;
may his gifts be despised of the gods,
may his altar-fires die out.

Epode   They are there,

they are there
on the height;
already they reach the peak
and the crag
of the rock, Parnassus;
they are there,
aloft,
in the high air,
where wild Bakkhos
carries the torch,
where Bacchantes
dance in the night;
God grant
that this boy perish;
God grant
that he die in his youth;

these strangers
have stolen our house
and the house
of the old King,
Erekhtheus.

THE QUEEN RETURNS, *in perhaps the most notable section of the drama, with an old man, one of those arch-types of classic art, a Job in dignity, antiquity itself, Saturn hobbling with a long staff; half-blind wisdom doomed to outlive its generation; he must be very old. We learn from the conversation that he was a teacher of the father of Kreousa.*

Perhaps the figure of the noble woman, as she appears with the old man, is the most striking of all her characterizations. In her abstract power, she seems now the very embodiment of that Virgin Mother of her city, Athené, strength, power, wisdom with the abstraction of Time, the grandfather, as it were, of her own brain-birth.

Curious words, these. How can we believe that 500 B.C. and A.D. 500 (or our own problematical present) are separated by an insurmountable chasm? The schism of before and after Christ, vanishes. The new modernity can not parody the wisdom of all-time with its before and after. The poet Euripides, one of that glorious trio of Athens' great dramatic period—the world's greatest—predicts the figure of the new world-woman; tenderness and gallantry merge in this Kreousa, who yearns in neurotic abandon for a child she has lost, yet at the same time retains a perfectly abstract sense of justice, of judgment toward the highest aesthetic religious symbol of the then known world. She questions the god, and she questions him with emotional fervour and with intellect. Her personality, her unity was violated by this god, by inspiration. She has accepted her defeat, yet has retained her integrity. At the moment of her entrance, she still believes in the justice of the old ideal.

Kreousa	Come with me,
	venerable and dear
	teacher of my father,
	come
	to this altar;
	we will rejoice together;
	Loxias will grant my wish;
	how can it be other?
	it is so sweet to have you here,

kind friend,
old teacher,
I love you,
(though I am your queen)
father;

Old Man

your words
are like your father's words,
noble,
ancestral;
you honour all the old ways,
earth-born daughter;
lead,
lead me to the portal;
stones hurt;
I am so old;
the way is steep
to the temple;

Kreousa

follow me;
look—

Old Man

my spirit flies,
not my feet—

Kreousa

here is your stick;
follow these rocks—

Old Man

my stick is as blind
as I—

Kreousa

my dear,
don't fall—

Old Man

are we almost
there?

Kreousa	here, stand my women; speak, friends of my loom and distaff; what does fate grant? what hope have we of that child for which we ask? speak; for good news, good gifts—
Choros	Daimon—
Kreousa	what?
Choros	alas—
Old Man	what is this, what unhappiness?
Choros	what do we hope but death?
Kreousa	why this— this plaint?
Choros	shall we speak or be silent?
Kreousa	speak— the worst—
Choros	I speak twice-death;

you may never press
that child
in your arms,
O, queen—

Kreousa   aye,
                death—

Old Man   dearest—

Kreousa   I am struck,
                hurt,
                slain—

Old Man   we are lost—

Kreousa   O, my heart—
                my heart—

Old Man   grieve not—

Kreousa   O, grief—

Old Man   let us learn—

Kreousa   learn? what?

Old Man   whether your husband,
                likewise
                is desolate—

Choros   O, old man,
                Loxias
                has given him,
                and him alone,
                a son—

Kreousa	what? this is the end—
Old Man	now living, or yet to come?
Choros	I have seen him, full-grown—
Kreousa	impossible— speak—
Old Man	what did it say, the Voice, (speak clearly) whose is this infant?
Choros	the youth he first met, as he came from the sacred gate, god gave him, for his son;
Kreousa	my palace is empty alas, and I am alone—
Old Man	whom did he meet? speak, speak; where did they meet and when?
Choros	O, lady, you saw the one who swept the temple? that is his son.

Kreousa	God grant that I disappear into thin air, God grant that I be carried far, far out of Hellas, God grant that I fall where the western stars fall, that I may no more suffer.
Old Man	what is his name? do you know?
Choros	he is called Ion, first-met;
Old Man	his mother?
Choros	we don't know; we only know how that father has gone off with his son for a sacrifice; they prepare a banquet in the sacred tent, to celebrate the son's return home;
Old Man	I weep with you, queen, this is theft and an insult;

we are bereft
of the house
of Erekhtheus;

Choros

I weep with you,
queen,
share your exile
and death.

Kreousa

Soul,
soul,
speak;
nay, soul, O, my soul,
be silent;
how can you name an act
of shame,
an illicit act?
soul,
soul,
be silent;
nay, nay, O, my soul,
speak;
what can stop you,
what can prevent?
is not your husband traitorous?
he has stolen your hope
and your house;
all hope of a child is lost;
great Zeus,
O, great Zeus,
be my witness;
O, goddess
who haunts my rocks,
by Tritonis
your holy lake,
be witness;
O, witness and help,
O, stars,
O, star-throne of Zeus;

I have hidden too long
this truth,
I must lighten my heart
of this secret;
I must be rid of it.

O, eyes,
eyes weep,
O, heart,
heart break,
you fell in a trap of men,
you were snared in a god's net;
(are gods or are men more base?)

O, eyes,
eyes weep,
O, heart,
O, my heart
cry out
against him of the seven-strung lyre,
against him of the singing voice;
yes,
to you, you, you
I shout,
harmony, rhythm, delight
of the Muses,
you I accuse;
you, born of Leto,
you bright
traitor within the light;

why did you seek me out,
brilliant, with gold hair? vibrant,
you seized my wrists,
while the flowers fell from my lap,
the gold and the pale-gold crocus,
while you fulfilled your wish;
what did it help, my shout

of mother,
mother?
no help
came to me
in the rocks;
O, mother,
O, white hands caught;
O, mother,
O, gold flowers lost;

O, terror,
O, hopeless loss,
O, evil union,
O, fate;
where is he whom you begot?
(for fear of my mother,
I left
that child
on those bride-rocks;)

O, eyes,
eyes weep,
but that god will not relent,
who thought of the harp-note
while his child was done to death
by hovering eagles or hawks;
O, heart,
heart break,
but your heart will never break,
who sit apart
and speak
prophecies;
I will speak
to you on your golden throne,
you devil
at earth-heart,
your golden tripod
is cursed;

O, evil lover,
you grant
my husband who owes you naught,
his child to inherit my house,
while my child
and your child
is lost;
our son was torn by beaks
of ravaging birds,
he was caught
out of the little robes
I wrapped him in,
and lost;

O, terror,
O, hopelessness,
O, evil union,
O, fate,
I left him there on the rocks,
alone
in a lonely place,
be witness,
O, Delos,
and hate,
hate him, O, you laurel-branch,
hate,
hate him
you palm-branch,
càught
with the leaves of the laurel to bless
that other so-holy birth,
yours,
Leto's child
with Zeus;

heart,
heart weep,

soul,
O, my soul,
cry out,
harmony, rhythm, delight
of the Muses,
you, I accuse
who pluck from the soulless frame of the
    harp,
the soul of the harp.

Choros　　　　　Terrible,
terrible
heart-break;
we, too, weep.

Old Man　　　　I am beside myself;
let me look,
let me look at your face;
your words
leave you breathless;
O, breathless,
they follow
in such haste;
I am done,
I am drowned;
O, my daughter,
evil follows
evil; disaster,
disaster;

what is it?
do you accuse
Loxias?
whose is this child
you lost?
where is that haunt
of wild beasts?

                    O, repeat,
                    repeat this—

Kreousa   I am ashamed,
                    yet speak—

Old Man   let me grieve
                    with your grief.

Again we have another of these long dialogues, to which no translation can do justice. There are roughly another hundred lines, of perfectly matched lyrical conversation; question and answer follow each other in the strictest rhythm and infallible regard to rule of metre and rhetoric; musically, this is the unquestioned classic method of a Bach or Haydn.

Dramatically?

We are back again with our old bag of tricks, we are re-working a pattern in a tapestry, we have heard all this before. The dialogue, at times, seems to play almost the same rôle as the prologue; the words may be monotonously chanted, when dramatic sequence allows; they may numb us into some state of affable acceptance; we need some sort of antidote to this high-pitched hysteria of perhaps the most ultra-modern of all this poet's lyric fragments.

The old man, as Fate's prompter, suggests a melodramatic solution to the predicament. Just kill your husband. The queen of Athens will not do this.

Kill the boy, then.

She agrees to this with suspicious alacrity.

She has loved this boy. She recognized psychic affinity at the first moment of their meeting. Her husband has been given a son by this Voice, that betrayed her in her girlhood. If the son had been any other than just that tall, curious, detached young foundling, to whom she had first spoken in the courtyard of the temple, she could have endured it; or if some other god, Bakkhos or even Zeus had oracularly given her husband that gift. She has been betrayed by God and man alike. Is the logic so flimsy? Is the psychological reasoning so weak? The much-quoted critic speaks of this woman as being a "savage" at heart. This is not the gesture of a frenzied, over-balanced woman. Kreousa retains, at the last her un-

*questionable authority. She is the nearest, in actual descent, to the
divinity of the Acropolis; her earth ancestor was born out of these very
stones, Athené lifted him up in her hands. That goddess was her foster-
mother, her intellectual progenitor. Kreousa, the woman, has failed, now
let Kreousa, the queen, speak.*

   *"I connive at this plot. I, as your regent, give you full authority to
strike at the enemy of my house."*

   *She hands the old man the magic poison that was the mystical gift
of the very goddess, to her race. She will save its authority, even if her city
Athens and all Attica is doomed to die with her.*

   *Kreousa, the queen, stands shoulder to shoulder with the sword-
bearer of the Acropolis. She, too, holds a weapon; she, too, strikes
infallibly at the enemy of her city. Kreousa, the queen, standing shoulder
to shoulder with Pallas Athené, becomes Kreousa, the goddess. The price?
Kreousa, the woman.*

Kreousa	—you know long-rocks?
Old Man	—you mean Pan's grot?
Kreousa	—yes; there I met—
Old Man	—speak; my heart breaks—
Kreousa	—fearful—alas—
Old Man	—yes, yes; I guess—
Kreousa	I must speak out—
Old Man	—sad, O sad secret—
Kreousa	—but now, no secret—
Old Man	—how did you hide it?
Kreousa	—wait; let me speak—

Old Man	—who helped with this?
Kreousa	—I had no help—
Old Man	—but where—where is it?
Kreousa	—the child? ah, wild beasts—
Old Man	—but the god saved it?
Kreousa	—the god? no—
Old Man	—who left the child?
Kreousa	—who? I—black night—
Old Man	—and who knew of it?
Kreousa	O, no one knew—
Old Man	—but you—how could you?
Kreousa	—how? my heart broke—
Old Man	—O, god's cruel heart—
Kreousa	—his small hands reached—
Old Man	—seeking your breast—
Kreousa	—seeking my breast—
Old Man	—what did you think?
Kreousa	—think? God will help—
Old Man	—alas, Erekhtheus—

Kreousa	—veil not your face—
Old Man	—your father's face—
Kreousa	—fate, fate—fate—fate—
Old Man	—weep not—weep not—
Kreousa	—but what is left?
Old Man	—revenge; strike—
Kreousa	—strike at the god?
Old Man	—burn this, his house—
Kreousa	—that will not help—
Old Man	—your husband, then—
Kreousa	—my bridegroom, no—
Old Man	—then, kill this child—
Kreousa	—what? ah—
Old Man	—a sword will serve—
Kreousa	I go—
Old Man	—on to the tent—
Kreousa	—but—no—
Old Man	—your courage fails?
Kreousa	—secret and sure—

Old Man	—what do you mean?
Kreousa	—from fight of giants—
Old Man	—yes, what of that?
Kreousa	—sprang monster Gorgo—
Old Man	—to fight the gods—
Kreousa	—but Pallas slew it—
Old Man	—that frightful form—
Kreousa	—those writhing serpents—
Old Man	—I've heard of it—
Kreousa	—Athené's aegis—
Old Man	—she wears the shield—
Kreousa	—among the gods—
Old Man	—but what of this?
Kreousa	—you know Erekhtheus?
Old Man	—your ancestor—
Kreousa	—Athené gave this—
Old Man	—yes, yes, speak clear—
Kreousa	—to him, a talisman—
Old Man	—and of what nature?

Kreousa	—blood-drops of magic—
Old Man	—strung on a necklace—
Kreousa	—in a gold amulet—
Old Man	—your father had it—
Kreousa	—and now, I have it—
Old Man	—how does it work?
Kreousa	—one blood-drop heals—
Old Man	—the other?
Kreousa	—slays—
Old Man	—are both together?
Kreousa	—can good and bad mix?
Old Man	—safe, safe at last—
Kreousa	—with the boy's death—
Old Man	O, let me help—
Kreousa	—when we get back—
Old Man	—no; here were best—
Kreousa	—in Athens, true—
Old Man	—you will be suspect—
Kreousa	—a step-mother—

Old Man   —accused of murder—

Kreousa   —yes, yes, yes, yes—

Old Man   —none shall guess this.

Kreousa   Take this amulet,
it is ancient
Athenian gold-work;
look for that secret place
where my husband
makes sacrifice;
there,
at the end of the feast,
as they lift
the libation-cup,
pour this,
(hidden
beneath your cloak)
into the boy's goblet;
but only into the one
of that would-be lord of my home;
one drop
and it is done;
and he shall never see Athens,
nor Athens see
that false son:

Old Man   and you,
go back to the town;
I'll see that all is done;
O, old, old feet,
you are strong;
what is age?
I shall strike again
a blow,
at those who have wronged

my lords;
I was old in my time
and wise;
but now,
now,
now
I am young.

XII

Aᴳᴬᴵᴺ *the choros marks time for us. We may imagine them now in their most abstract mood; their dark scarves drawn tight, they are the dark or sombre hours; they call upon the witch-woman who dwells at cross-roads, she who guides the murderer's hand, the instigator of hidden magic. This is good old classic melodrama. Nothing is spared us. Let the blood of the dragon in the magic filtre slay this youth, for if he lives, our mistress will not. She will hang herself, she will plunge a dagger into her heart and so on.*

As I say, the choros is the march-past of hours, their time-values are ultra-modern, accordion-pleated, as it were. They may minimize the passage of time, or in a few stark words, they may convey an impression of hours lapsed. Here, we are made to realize the actual setting of the doomed feast. And the choros of witch-women, now taking tone from their queen, the leader of their moods and emotions, reviles the sun-god. Who is he, anyway? No such things, we can imagine them thinking, ever happen in our holy city. There, intellect, justice, integrity rule, and gods and men step forth to prescribed formula. This sun-god had mixed the vibrations, has committed that most dire of spiritual sins, he has played fast and loose with the dimension of time and space. He appeared for a whim, to a girl, and that girl, their queen; and, for a whim, deserted her. A god should know his place, all values have been reversed. And does this pretender, this waif, know what it's all about? And now the poet himself forgets this threnody in his sheer delight of words; they again seduce him, as it were, in spite of himself—or in spite of these doleful hours—into a by-play of vibrant images, dance, sea-floor, stars, a gold crown, a Virgin.

This poet's golden images seep up, inevitably; they are like treasure seen far, far down under black, sweeping storm-waves.

Choros	Demeter's
Strophe I	daughter,
	mistress of cross-ways,
	Hecate,
	step forth;
	yourself,
	yourself

mix the cup,
preside
at the feast of death;
fill the goblet,
with blood-drops
of the earth-born
dragon,
(in that tent,
as our queen directs),
for him
who would steal our house;
for no stranger may pass
our gate,
as a king,
none rule
but a child
of Erekhtheus;

Antistrophe I   for this is the end
of us all,
if the plot fail,
the end of our queen;
she will pierce,
with a sword,
a vein;
she will knot
a cord,
a halter
about her throat;
she will seek life
in another place;
not here;
this sun-light shall not fall
on an outcast,
an alien,
thrust
from her own door;

Strophe II

too much is said of this god,
too much is sung,
too much of the sacred spring;
what of deeds in the night?
will that boy ever know?
will he see what the torch-flame saw?

will he watch the stars on high,
the moon and the moon-dance?
will he wonder?
will he witness
the sea-dance,
fifty Neriads,
in and out
of the sea-wave,
on the sea-floor?

will he worship,
adore
the Virgin,
gold-crowned,
and the holy Mother?

this waif,
from a temple,
would steal,
betray,
take
the throne
of another.

XIII

THE DISHEVELLED *forward-rush of a servant tells us what we already know, what we have known for a long time. Kreousa's plot must fail. Here is another time-worn device of classic drama, this servant is the familiar Messenger, who shares with the prologue, as a rule, the honour of holding the stage longest. The Messenger is to the end, or the middle-end of the drama, what the prologue is to the beginning. Infallibly, he picks up threads that have already been woven and re-woven, finds loose ends, unravels here and there and re-weaves, till there can be no possible loose-stitch, no blur in the out-line, no rough seam, no hint of clumsy handiwork. Indeed, the Attic drama was fitly presided over, by that patron alike of all subtle spinners and thinkers, Pallas Athené.*

Servant	Women, where is your mistress, daughter of Erekhtheus? I have looked here, there, everywhere in the town;
Choros	what— what is it, O slave? what do you want?
Servant	they're after her— she's to be flung from the precipice—
Choros	speak— (have we been found out?)
Servant	I heard that— yes, you're in it—
Choros	but the plot— who discovered it?

Servant	the god;
	does he rank evil
	above justice?
	it was his act—

Choros	yes,
	yes,
	but quick, tell us,
	do we live?
	is life our fate?
	or death?
	do we die?

Servant	They left the temple, they came:
	to the festive place, where priests:
	prepared the altar, where burnt:
	the fire of the god Bakkhos:
	there, Xouthos rendered thanks:
	for his son:
	he stained the rocks:
	with the victims for Dionysos:
	the husband of Kreousa spoke:
	now set the tent upright:
	I visit the gods of birth:
	if I am late, invite:
	the guests, begin the feast:
	he took the votive beasts:
	he went; the boy set up:
	the tent-poles, fastened taut:
	the cloth, to shield from heat:
	of noon or the setting-sun;
	a plethron long, square-shaped:
	the whole stretched out, firm set:
	a thousand feet, a room:
	for the Delphic people's feast:
	and now he covered it:
	with the temple-treasure, stuffs:

beautifully wrought with work:
from the Amazons; on the roof:
was the cloth-wing Heracles brought:
as spoil to the house of Phoibos:
Ouranos shone on the cloth:
the sun drove the sun-chariot:
to the west, with the star Hesperus:
the moon, dark-clad, went forth:
with her steeds unyoked; aloft:
stars wheeled; Pleiads, the giant:
with sword-hilt, Orion, and last:
the Bear turned his length round a
    north-pole:
of gold, while Selene shot bright:
rays for each month; and the tempest:
stars, Hyades, gleamed till the luminous:
Dawn drove the stars back:

moreover, he fastened yet:
more beautiful cloth; strange ships:
enemy-oars fight Greeks:
there are men, half-man, half-beast:
and a deer and a wild-lion hunt:
Kekrops with his brood by the entrance:
curved his tail; some Athenian's gift:
and here, in the midst of the tent:
they placed gold kraters; a legate:
stretched to his height, blew a blast;
on the trumpet, to call to the feast:
all Delphi; when all was placed:
they served them, they crowned them, and
    last:
a very old man came up:
to greet them; he made them laugh:
with his curious gestures; he helped:
pour water, he lit sweet-myrrh:
he made himself wine-butler:

with the flutes, he ordered the last:
great, gold-wrought, thanks-giving cups:
he selected the finest goblet:
hail, our new master; he dropped:
poison, (none knew of this) the queen's
    gift:
into the cup; as the youth lifted it up:
in prayer, a servant spoke:
an ill-omened word; as priests':
companion, himself, a priest:
the youth interpreted this:
bring a fresh krater; he spilt:
his wine and invited the guests:
likewise, to empty theirs out:
as libation, unto the earth:
in silence, fresh wine was brought:
mixed Byblos; doves from the gate:
flew in; they are safe in the court:
of the temple; they dipped their beaks:
in the poured-out wine, flung back:
their feathered throats; one dropped:
shuddering, at the youth's feet:
it beat its wings, it wept:
the guests stood up, alas:
it stiffened; its purple feet:
curled under, in death:

who has attempted this? (the boy:
the oracle's choice, flung back his robe:
leapt up); speak, speak, old man:
you sought my death, the cup came from
    your hand:
he caught the old man by the arm:
surprised in the very act:
he confessed the sacrilege, Kreousa:
the amulet; the young priest rushed out:
with the guests, to the place of judgment:

O, sacred earth, be witness:
and you, O, Pythian fathers:
(he spoke to the court) a stranger:
the daughter of Erekhtheus:
has sought my death:
their vote was unanimous:
the lords of Delphi spoke:
she plotted against a priest:
she would have taken his life:
and in the sacred House:
let her be hurled from the rocks:

now the whole town is out:
your mistress came to this place:
to ask from its god, birth:
he commands death.

A SHORT *lyrical rhapsody, or threnody, from the choros, after the smooth narrative of the Messenger, reminds one of the first appearance of Ion, and his outcry against the birds from Parnassus. We remember how he aimed his arrow, at the same time uttering a prayer for the safety of winged messengers of God. Like an old nordic wood-tale or myth of folk-lore, the bird whom our hero had propitiated in the beginning, in the end, saves him. It is a dove, who, according to divine pattern, offers himself as sacrifice.*

There is a waywardly mystical tone in this classic writer as if he, like his hero-dæmon or god-villain, had mixed time and space, played fast and loose with convention of here-and-now. A later Byzantine writer might have invoked this image of a bird slain for a human-spirit, or the most vibrant of Augustine Latins might have been criticized for being over-ornate with this mixed imagery, taste, sight, colour, a white bird we presume, with its breast stained scarlet. The flock of birds seems intrusion from one of those spice-islands of the great lyric period of Greek poetry— with their voices, we see palm-shadows, the grape itself is not more intoxicating to our senses than, to our sight, the sway and delicate fluttering, as they group around the wine-pool. On my visit to Delphi, I was surprised to find coral-branches of our so-called Judas-tree, cutting irregular, jagged purple against the weathered masonry of ruined porches. Here is the same shock, as of an intrusion, against lined marble and stark Doric column, of the most exotic of eastern patterns; fragrance, colour, taste—as if the poet had, inadvertently, spilled wine-purple through the pure line-ing of his own verse.

Choros	Now is there nothing left;
	for us, it is manifest,
	hers
	is our death;
	a dove was the cause of it;
	with the sweet of the vine,
	he tasted
	the blood-drop
	of death;

alas,
my life;
alas,
my mistress;
she shall be hurled
from Parnassus;
would I had wings
and could fly;
would I could creep
through the earth;
they will stone me
to death;

O, for a chariot,
O, for a ship—
escape;
can a god help?
O, most unhappy
mistress,
what is your punishment?
there is one law,
one judgment;
he who plans ill
for another,
must himself,
suffer it.

XV

ACCORDING *to immemorial Greek law, a fugitive may take shelter at the altar of the god. Especially was this so at Delphi, high court of justice, both political and ecclesiastical. We may still run our fingers over stones, read with our spirit a sort of immortal Braille, that informs us of this and that slave, purchased back from his master, with his own earnings, or escaped or given to the god, presented with his own freedom, in other words, as a token of love and trust, by a former owner. Because of this immemorial tradition of the right of the fugitive, the attendant ladies of the queen urge her, on her frantic, hunted entrance, to take shelter by the altar. In this two-edged Delphi there was civil law—but over and beyond it was, definitely, a law we too often arrogantly claim as peculiar to our own times, the law of mercy.*

Kreousa	I must die, I am caught, they condemn me to death—
Choros	we know, O unhappy woman, alas—
Kreousa	I escaped the town, but what use? I am lost—
Choros	the altar—
Kreousa	can that help?
Choros	a suppliant— you are safe—
Kreousa	but the law decrees —death

Choros	the god's law protects—
Kreousa	they come— see—their spears—
Choros	but quick, mount the step, stand there by the altar; if fate will, you escape, he who strikes, will be banished.

XVI

Ion had accepted second-best and he knew it. Nevertheless, the mortal youth was intoxicated with a sudden insight into mundanity. His foster-father was a wealthy and distinguished soldier, of a renowned family, not an Athenian, to be sure, but for all that, a stalwart member of the old aristocracy. The boy who had yearned all his life for the mere come and go of ordinary people, of ordinary human contacts, was suddenly overwhelmed by this brilliant festival. The sacrifice, at its inception, to the god, was by way of a decorative convention, part of the banquet, not really savouring of those old ritual ceremonies, in the temple, that had lain all those brilliant hours far, far down below in the valley, at his feet. He had climbed high, in a moment; and what is this mere legal question anyhow, of parentage worth, we can imagine him asking himself, as the procession of musicians and court-entertainers pass before him. It is conceivable that Xouthos had brought with him his personal body-guard from Athens, and the formality of their acceptance of the adopted son of their chief must have been overwhelming. His head has been turned in a moment.

Was he not, at heart, the son of that luxury-loving, yet totally vibrant and detached musician? Did Ion not feel, at last, that the old ritual was out-worn and those priests and pythonesses of his childhood, antique mummers and old dolls? Here was life, living.

In a moment, it was to be swept from him.

At the exact second, as his hand reached out, and his material body was to be sworn-in as it were, to a brotherhood of mastery and battle, the hand drops.

There is a greater brotherhood.

He does not yet know this.

He only sees a woman cowering by an altar. Her veil is torn. Who is she? Of course; the change is startling but that is what she was like, always. The image of the tragic, stark-eyed queen whom he had first met in this very courtyard, has shrunk. She is, after all, only another failure. Perhaps his own soul, still recognizing their actual spirit affinity, for that reason, the more reviled her. He too, in a moment, would be dragged back into this psychic hinterland of loss, doubt, loss of personal identity, loss of mundanity, loss of material position, that terrible groping depersonalization of all true sons of the sun-god, music, and inspiration.

He shouts at her, in anger; he drags out invective. His manner is over-done. It is necessary to over-compensate, over-stress, over-act his part. For it is only a part he is acting, and he, unconsciously, must know it.

But Kreousa, on the other hand, has found something that all the time was there. In spite of invective against her lover, in spite of the recurrent motif of loss and desertion, in spite of the reiteration, the accusing tirade, was she too, like her own son, arguing down something in her own spirit, rather than inveighing against mere outside circumstance? It seems now, we guess for the first time, that the spark lit by her lordly lover had never really gone out. She clings to the laurel-branches on the altar and she clearly gets the better of her son, in this argument: what is the god to you? *he asks. She says,* my body is his by right, *and even more significantly,* I am safe with the god.

Would Kreousa of Athens, virgin and queen, at last analysis, have chosen a lesser lover than the lord of light?

Ion

O face of a monster,
what dragon begot you?
what devil,
what flame?
your evil is worse
than that Gorgon
whose blood-drop
was your weapon:

catch her;
she shall lie at the base
of the mountain,
Parnassus;
her hair
shall be torn
on its crags;

my good Dæmon was near me,
it heard me,
it saved me

from this,
a step-mother
and strangers,
the insult of Athenians;
away from my friends,
I had entered her trap;
she had done me to death;

and now do you think
that the altar will save you,
the laurel, the temple?

you weep?
tears are due
my own mother
(I never forget her)
not you;

look how she shakes,
trick upon trick,
no prayer
shall avail you.

Kreousa	I am safe with the god;
Ion	what is the god to you?
Kreousa	my body is his, by right;
Ion	who would have killed his priest;
Kreousa	you are your father's, not his;
Ion	I was always his near-son;
Kreousa	you were—but my day has come;
Ion	you are his in crime, I, in beauty;

Kreousa	I fought the enemy of my own city;
Ion	I came, didn't I, with a mighty army?
Kreousa	you did, to destroy the house of Erekhtheus;
Ion	—what flame, what torch?
Kreousa	—dishonesty, theft—
Ion	—my father's gift—
Kreousa	—*his*—the city of Pallas?
Ion	—his sword saved it—
Kreousa	—he never owned it—
Ion	—you feared my future—
Kreousa	—your death or my death—
Ion	—you envy my father—
Kreousa	—you steal from the childless—
Ion	—my father's property—
Kreousa	—a sword, a spear—
Ion	—let go the altar—
Kreousa	—so? find your own mother—
Ion	—you'll pay for this—

Kreousa	—on the altar-step?
Ion	why should you wish to die mid the laurel-wreaths?
Kreousa	so I may grieve One who brought me grief;
Ion	this is preposterous; O, it is not right that evil should crouch in this marble, holy place; only the saintliest hands should touch the laurel; only the priests, by right, should mount this stair; away, away with her—

XVII

BUT THIS *is too much. The boy-priest, that detached spirit, who in the opening scene of this drama had been invoking pure-spirit in the heaven and praying for the very lives of those whom he was forced to slay, is crying out against that most ancient and remotely sacred of all religious institutions, that unquestioning right of the fugitive, king or beggar, slave or general, to ask, if luck grants him the will to get there, help, with the last gasp of his earthly body, of the inviolable altar of justice-beyond-justice. Luck or the god had willed that this queen find foot-hold on the rim of the altar, strength to climb that stair, breath to cry out her right to the indubitable protection of the divinity. And this youth, formerly so remote, so holy, so removed from all evil contact, his whole life one hymn of praise to the deity, must thwart her. He may question the right of the sun to rise by day and the stars by night but not the right of the fugitive to demand pity of the god. This right is immemorial and immemorial votaries guard it. Such a one, steps forth.*

"I am the Pythian priestess," she says. The boy falls back. There is no higher title, not one more honoured, in the whole civilized world. "I have been honoured of Phoibos, and I speak."

She is not young, this woman. It was against the veils of her early novitiate that those small hands had clung. The frozen body of the deserted waif was warmed before the brazier, burning in the inner-temple. His feet and hands were laved with holy water. And by whom? By the Pythoness of Delphi.

No slight honour for a mortal; even if he had been that, these ministrations would have conferred immortality upon him. Ion can struggle no longer with the fate that proffers him divinity. He bows his head, "mother," he says, "of my spirit."

The Pythia	No;
	peace;
	I,
	prophetess,
	honoured of Phoibos,
	first among all the women of Delphi,

chosen
to protect
the temple's
ancient rites,

I,
even I
left the tripod,
stand here,
speak:

Ion	mother of my spirit:
Pythia	mother; the name is sweet:
Ion	you have heard of this woman's plot?
Pythia	I have, but are you blameless?
Ion	I struck at a murderess:
Pythia	she was wounded, a stricken wife:
Ion	more—a vengeful step-mother
Pythia	no: my son, leave this place:
Ion	how? what have I in life?
Pythia	Athens; go with pure heart:
Ion	to strike at evil, is pure:
Pythia	you must know why you strike:
Ion	was I wrong? are you right?
Pythia	look at this old box:

Ion	a basket, with faded fillets:
Pythia	you were left here in this:
Ion	what? impossible—speak—
Pythia	I reveal things, long secret:
Ion	but why have you hidden this?
Pythia	it was the god's wish:
Ion	and now, what does he ask?
Pythia	having found your father, depart:
Ion	who told you to keep the basket?
Pythia	the Voice spoke to my spirit:
Ion	and asked what? what?
Pythia	that the basket be given back:
Ion	for what good or what evil purpose?
Pythia	all your little things are here:
Ion	to help me to find my mother?
Pythia	when god wills, not before:
Ion	O, day, O, too luminous:
Pythia	take this; search carefully for her; do everything yourself,

neglect no spot
in Asia,
search all Europe
for your mother;
I love you;
it is the god's wish,
dear child,
that I give you back
this:
(O, how carefully
I have kept it);

I do not know why
the god asks this;
no one in the whole world
knew I had it,
nor where I hid the box;

hail;
I have loved you
as much as any mother,
yet
you must find her;
first, ask here;
some Delphic girl
might have
left her child
on these steps;
ask of the Greeks;

this is my last command
(the god speaks
through me),
farewell.

XVIII

SHE HAS GONE, *that most beautiful wraith, that ghost from antiquity, and the boy's uneven duality must cry out in agony as he seeks to find the balance between the detached introversion of the temple servant and the dream of easy mundanity, power and human delight. There is a third Ion to be born from the struggle of these two, the Ion whose power is predicted by the speaker of the prologue, a spirit yet a man, the founder of distant colonies, the protector and progenitor of Greek culture throughout Asia and the world. From Ion the spirit and Ion the mortal, is born a third, compound of man and god, Ion, the Ionian.*

But this birth, like all birth, is physically painful, and spiritually heart-breaking.

He holds a painted box in his lap, bound with old cords, faded fillets or ribbons.

Like a child with a box of toys from one dead, his head falls forward on the painted lid.

Ion, the Ionian, will be born of this box, but the youth in painful state of transition, now asks, who am I? After all, this parade on the hill-top may turn out to be the most humiliating and ironical of farces. I may be the child of the meanest slave in the lowest quarter of the outer town of Delphi or even from some malsain *village, further along the sea-coast, he thinks. Then he opens the box.*

Ion   And now,
                 I weep;
                 think;
                 my own mother
                 (secret bride)
                 hid me in this very box;
                 I never touched her breast;

                 I am nameless;
                 I really lived a slave's life
                 in this place:

                 true,
                 the god,

always was exquisite;
the rest?
bad luck;

O, all those years
lost;
mother—

how she must have suffered;

O, my cradle,
I offer you to the god,
(although I am yet ignorant,
as to whether I am a slave's son;
perhaps it will be worse
to find that mother,
than not);

Helios,
I consecrate this
in your precinct;
what shall I do next?
I must do what he asks;
I must look inside it;
I must open the basket;
I dare not fight
fate;

O, sacred fillets,
why were you kept
from me?
O, cords
round the basket,
what have you hidden?

how fair,
this basket,
so carefully kept—
for what?

Kreousa	you—you—there—
Ion	O, quiet—away—do not touch—
Kreousa	no, no, no, give it back; it's my child's basket—
Ion	she is mad, catch her—
Kreousa	kill me rather— I don't care; I will have it, and all the little things in it— my basket—
Ion	she is terrible with her lies—
Kreousa	no; thank you, thank you, too, you've helped— you, you dear—
Ion	dear? but just now, you wanted to kill—
Kreousa	I didn't know, I didn't know you—

Ion	tricks, more tricks—
Kreousa	I can prove—
Ion	and I; what's in this basket?
Kreousa	your little dresses—
Ion	very well, but what?
Kreousa	O, I can't speak—
Ion	speak; you seem to know—
Kreousa	there's a blanket, my own embroidery—
Ion	what's on it?
Kreousa	I didn't even finish it—
Ion	well, what's the pattern?
Kreousa	I began a Gorgon, in the middle—
Ion	God—
Kreousa	then, there're serpents round it, like an aegis—

Ion   yes,
                 here it is—

Kreousa   O,
                 childhood
                 task—

Ion   what else?

Kreousa   dragons
                 of gold-work—

Ion   the charm
                 of Athené—

Kreousa   in memory
                 of Erekhtheus—

Ion   what are they for?

Kreousa   a sort of necklace—

Ion   it's here—
                 but there's one thing more—

Kreousa   yes,
                 there's one thing more;

                 O, olive
                 of Athens,
                 O, crown of wild-olives,
                 I plucked
                 from the very holy rock;
                 it is sacred;
                 the very branch,
                 the goddess herself
                 brought;

it never loses its silver
immortal
leaf;
it is there;

Ion

mother,
my mother,
most dear—

Kreousa

son,
O, light,
more lovely than Helios
(and the god will pardon this),
you are in my arms
at last,
I had thought you lost,
long ago,
with the ghosts
in death—

Ion

alive
and dead,
both—

Kreousa

Io;
what cry is there,
what joy from the lips
can answer
the joy in my heart?
Io;
speed joy
through the luminous
high air:

Ion

this has happened
more swiftly
than thought—

Kreousa	I tremble still with terror—
Ion	did you ever dream of this?
Kreousa	dream? where is the prophetess? I would ask who brought you here—
Ion	be happy, why ask? it was the god's wish—
Kreousa	how did I bring you forth? O, tears— how did I let you go? I breathe at last—
Ion	I, too—
Kreousa	mine is no barren house; Erekhtheus puts forth a branch and flowers; the earth-born race again sees light; O, light, Helios—
Ion	my father must know of this—
Kreousa	your father?
Ion	why not?

Kreousa	you had another father—
Ion	alas—
Kreousa	hymen which gave you life, had no torch-procession, no chant—
Ion	I am ill-begot—
Kreousa	let Pallas speak—
Ion	what?
Kreousa	ah, she who sits on my rocks, she knows, Pallas of the olive-branch—
Ion	speak out—
Kreousa	on the Acropolis, haunted of nightingales, Phoibos—
Ion	why Phoibos?
Kreousa	I was his bride—
Ion	fate— speak—
Kreousa	I had (in the tenth month)

                    the secret child—
                    of Helios—

Ion   if true—
                    how sweet—

Kreousa   only a girl,
                    a mother,
                    I wrapped him up
                    in this—
                    look, I embroidered it—
                    and you—
                    why, it was you—
                    you never touched my breast—
                    I couldn't even wash
                    your little feet,
                    I left you alone in the desert
                    for foraging hawks
                    and death—

Ion   how could you?

Kreousa   I was mad,
                    I might have killed you—

Ion   and I might have
                    murdered
                    you—

Kreousa   it's over,
                    don't speak of it—

Choros   let no man despair
                    after this—

Ion   but mother,
                    I hate to speak,

but—
tell me the truth;
O, tell me,
I'll understand;
you loved secretly,
were afraid,
said a god—

Kreousa   no,
by Athené Niké,
by Victory
and her chariot,
by her battle for Zeus
against giants,
I swear:
no mortal was your father,
only this king,
your protector,
Loxias—

Ion   why did he give
away
his son
to Xouthos?

Kreousa   he entrusted you
to a king,
as a man may make his friend,
his child's
guardian—

Ion   I doubt—

Kreousa   stop;
you dare not doubt;
Helios wanted you
to reign in a noble house;

he can not give you your birth-right,
his name,
as father;
O, don't you see?
even I,
even I,
overwrought,
wanted to kill you;
it was he
who watched over you—

no;
this is impossible;
I'll go to the temple,
I'll ask the oracle,
whether I am a god's son
or a mortal—

but
look—
there on the roof,
by the pinnacle,
hide your face,
hide your face,
mother,
it's dangerous—

a Presence
descends,
there,
there,
a Dæmon;

O, God,
O, Goddess,
O, face,
like the face
of Helios.

XIX

AND LAST *but not least,* deus ex machina *steps forth; intellect, mind, silver but shining with so luminous a splendour that the boy starts back, confusing this emanation of pure-spirit with that other, his spirit-father, her actual brother of Olympos. "Flee not," says Pallas Athené, "you flee no enemy in me," and this most beautiful abstraction of antiquity and of all time, pleas for the great force of the under-mind or the unconscious that so often, on the point of blazing upward into the glory of inspirational creative thought, flares, by a sudden law of compensation, down, making for tragedy, disharmony, disruption, disintegration, but in the end, O, in the end, if we have patience to wait, she says, if we have penetration and faith and the desire actually to follow all those hidden subterranean forces, how great is our reward. "You flee no enemy in me, but one friendly to you," says the shining intellect, standing full armed, in a silver that looks gold in the beams, as we may now picture them, of the actual sun, setting over the crags and pinnacles of Parnassus, shedding its subdued glow upon this group, these warm people who yet remain abstraction; a woman, her son; the haunting memory of a wraith-like priestess; the old, old man; the worldly king and general; the choros, so singularly a unit yet breaking occasionally apart, like dancers, to show individual, human Athenian women of the period, to merge once more into a closed circle of abstract joy or sorrow; the boy again in his manifold guises; the woman who is queen and almost goddess, who now in her joy wishes to be nothing but the mother of Ion; the mother, if she but knew it, of a new culture, of an æsthetic drive and concentrated spiritual force, not to be reckoned with, in terms of any then known values; hardly, even today, to be estimated at its true worth. For this new culture was content, as no culture had been before, or has since been, frankly with one and but one supreme quality, perfection. Beyond that, below it and before it, there was nothing. The human mind dehumanized itself, in much the same way (if we may imagine group-consciousness so at work) in which shell-fish may work outward to patterns of exquisite variety and unity. The conscious mind of man had achieved kinship with unconscious forces of most subtle definition. Columns wrought with delicate fluting, whorls of capitals, folds of marble garment, the heel of an athlete or the curls of a god or hero, the head-band of a high-priest or a goddess, the elbow-joint of* an archer or the lifted knee of one of the horses of the dioscuri, no matter how dissimilar, had yet one fundamental inner force that framed them, projected them, as (we repeat) a certain genus of deep-sea fish may project its shell. Shell, indeed, left high and dry when the black tide of late Rome and the Middle Ages had drawn far, far out, dragging man and man's æsthetic effort with it. A scattered handful of these creatures or creations is enough to mark, for all time, that high-water mark of human achievement, the welding of strength and delicacy, the valiant yet totally unselfconscious withdrawal of the personality of the artist, who traced on marble, for all time, that thing never to be repeated, faintly to be imitated, at its highest, in the Italian quattrocento, that thing and that thing alone that we mean, when we say, Ionian.

Let not our hearts break before the beauty of Pallas Athené. No; she makes all things possible for us. The human mind today pleads for all; nothing is misplaced that in the end may be illuminated by the inner fire of abstract understanding; hate, love, degradation, humiliation, all, all may be examined, given due proportion and dismissed finally, in the light of the mind's vision. Today, again at a turning-point in the history of the world, the mind stands, to plead, to condone, to explain, to clarify, to illuminate; and, in the name of our magnificent heritage of that Hellenic past, each one of us is responsible to that abstract reality; silver and unattainable yet always present, that spirit again stands holding the balance between the past and the future. What now will we make of it?

And how will we approach it? Not merely through subtle and exquisite preoccupations with shells of its luminous housing; no. Long ago, an olive-tree sprang up. It was sheltered by the Erechtheum. It was worshipped by virgin choros, procession of children, boys and girls; by the older girls; by the wise men of the city; by the heroes about to depart for Marathon; by poet and sculptor, king and visiting prelate. The Persian swept down on the city. We all know of this. We know how not one stone was left upon another, how the old wooden temple that held the ancient dragon and the smiling, ironical, thin and fragile goddess herself, striking it back, fell charred, and buried beneath it, other priceless images, a thin Dioskouros mounting to a horse, a weathered Hermes, a Victory, a stone owl, a plaque, inscribed with legal matter, dating from the days of Solon. The mighty olive-tree had been planted by the very hands of the goddess; it was this gift to men that the gods had placed above the *inestimable offering of Poseidon's white, swift horses. The olive was beautiful and useful, it fed and gave that oil, prized alike for food, for anointing Pythian or Isthmian victor, and for ritualistic sacrifice. The charred stump of the tree stood out now among the ruins of the Acropolis. "When our olive-tree dies," the Athenians had been taught from childhood, "our city is lost." Ah lost—lost city!*

Tradition has it that one devote scrambled back. He was disobedient to the injunction of his goddess, blatantly for this one time, rebellious. Of nothing, too much. Of one thing too much, and for the last time, that one thing (we may imagine his tense thought, valiant above his broken heart-beats) beauty. Not the beauty of the lyre-note plucked at dawn, not the beauty of ecstasy of the red-wine cup and song among the dancers, not the beauty of the virgin-huntress knee-deep in wild lilies, not the beauty of the cloudy outline (God of men, of gods) your father, O Athené, resting on the hill-tops; not snow, nor cloud, nor thunder, nor wind, nor rain, nor the concrete projected reality of stone coping nor architrave, but the beauty of pure thought—and he would fall here—his ankles burnt with smouldering beams from the little, painted ark-temple; his torn sandals were scorched, his heart beating, his last heart-beat. O yes, he can remember them, his friends in the little, lost city. They are strapping their miserable bundles, trying to fasten overcrowded or almost empty boxes, ready to flee the Persian, the Persian—lost—we can share his thought, feel the vibration of his rebellion, of nothing too much— *save of this thing. Our love for our lost city.*

There was a new war plague that year with a new name, but his lungs and his knees have come this far to defy her injunction (with his last breath) of nothing too much. And there by the charred stump of the old, of the immemorial olive, we may hear his last cry. Of this thing, too much—

Did he sleep, our rebellious Athenian? What dawn saw him rise? How was he wakened? By cold wind, no doubt, from the sea, that blue sea that, always its traditional enemy, had now deserted Athens for good. Poseidon had won at last. He might easily have sunk the straits in white foam, or better, summoned an earthquake to fling up rock bulwarks against the invading splendour of those purple galleys. The sea did not listen to the propitiatory prayers of the holy denizens of his city. He sent no storm to wreck the enemies of Greece—and yet he, too, was Greek.

Faithless and treacherous at the last, he seemed even to encourage with tender sea-breeze the freightage of these robbers. And what had the west to give them that the east had not? Laden with gold and packed with their beaten goblets, the galleys of Xerxes sought wealth here (O, little, ark-like, painted temple of wisdom!) worth all their fabulous trappings, harness for a million stallion, tent-poles of gold, awnings fringed with silver, gold-pricked tapestries. From Athens' ancient enemy, the sea, the dawn came.

Our Athenian's face was black with ashes, so that what he saw was, no doubt, part of the dishevelled humour of his dreaming. He reached out his frozen hand toward the charred stump of the once sacred olive-tree, to find—

Close to the root of the blackened, ancient stump, a frail silver shoot was clearly discernible, chiselled as it were, against that blackened wood; incredibly frail, incredibly silver, it reached toward the light. Pallas Athené, then, was not dead. Her spirit spoke quietly, a very simple message.

How did he get back to his people? What did he say when he finally overtook them, perhaps on the old, sacred Eleusinian highway? What was their answer to the rapture of his so simple, so spiritual message, that told his companions of that hope (from which sprang a later Parthenon). Our old tree is not dead. The Persian has not killed it.

Today? Yesterday? Greek time is like all Greek miracles. Years gain no permanence nor impermanence by a line of curious numbers; numerically 1920, 1922 and again (each time, spring) 1932, we touched the stem of a frail sapling, an olive-tree, growing against the egg-shell marble walls of the Erechtheum.

While one Ionic column stands, stark white and pure on the earth, that name shall live, the power of the goddess shall not have passed, the beauty and the cruelty of her brother shall not be relegated as sheer dæmonism or paganism (whatever, God help us, that word has come to mean), while one Ionic column lives to tell of the greatest æsthetic miracle of all-time, welding of beauty and strength, the absolute achievement of physical perfection by the spirit of man, before the world sank into the darkness of late Rome and the Middle Ages, this goddess lives.

Flee not,

---

in me
you flee no enemy,
but one friendly to you,
Pallas.

Athené   Flee not,
in me
you flee no enemy,
but one friendly to you,
Pallas;
I come from Athens
in my chariot;
I am sent
by Helios
who fears your reproach;
that is past;

I speak
for Helios;

he is your father;
he gave you to another
so that you might enter
a noble house;
but fearing
(once found out)
that your mother

might slay you,
or you slay your mother,
he sent me;

he would keep this secret;
the Athenians must not know;

but for you,
I fastened my steeds

to my chariot,
for you,
I came
to reveal
mystery;

Kreousa,
go home;
place your own child
on his
and on your throne.

Ion   Pallas,
great daughter of Zeus,
how could one question
you?
how could one doubt
your speech?
what was impossible before,
is clear;
I am the son
of Loxias;

Kreousa   now you must listen,
I speak,
I praise
whom I blamed,
Helios;
he has repaid
my loss;
O, doors,
O, oracular gates,
you were black before,
now
what light,
what light
breaks;

O, handle,
I touch you,
I kiss you,
O, holy door;

Athené the gods' pace moves slow,
do they forget?
no;
blessed be the man
who waits
(nor doubts)
for the end
of the intricate
plan.

Kreousa O, child,
come home—

Athené lead on,
I follow—

Ion what friends,
what a road—

Kreousa lead
to Athens—

Athené and a throne—

Ion for me,

ION

Choros Apollo,
son of Zeus,
son of Leto,

hail,
hail,
O, Apollo;

and you, too,
praise the gods,
that your heart may be free
and your home;

if you love the gods,
you too,
shall be loved of fate;

but you evil
doubter,
you shall be
desolate.

NOTE ON THE TEXT

In 1954 H. D. reread her *Ion* translation, and the present text incorporates the emendations H. D. then made in her copy of the 1937 printing (published by Chatto & Windus), subsequently given to Norman Holmes Pearson and presently in the Collection of American Literature, Beinecke Rare Book and Manuscript Library, Yale University—whose courteous help is thankfully noted.

THE OPENING SCENES OF ION

I

THIS PLAY of Euripides opens as is customary, with a long prologue. The prologue (apart from the beauty of the language) is in itself a rather tedious affair. As most people who read Greek a little, start, as is natural, at the beginning of a play, they are as naturally bored, and usually do not finish the prologue and conclude forever after if they are honest, that a Greek play is a bore. Or if they continue and finish, they are depressed throughout the drama, by the memory of the struggle and the weight of that ponderous beginning. The beginning is meant to be ponderous, it is more or less purposely boring.

The chief characters are named; the plot as in a grand-opera programme, briefly outlined.

The Athenian playgoer knew then from the start who would enter, what was about to take place. He came from his house, his regiment, from civic, social or political duties. "Of nothing, too much." The Athenian citizen was not to be jerked suddenly from one world to another. Life was to merge with art. But it was to merge, to be bridged gradually.

The long prologue was this bridge.

Though Attic tragedy was above all religious in purport, then (as in our own picture-theaters or grand-opera auditoriums) there must have been whisperings and shufflings and a general atmosphere of unrest at the beginning of a play.

Although we may visualize the actor, the speaker of the prologue, as having already entered, introducing himself as Hermes, the messenger, son of Maia and of the "greatest daemon, Zeus," the young aristocrat, Caierophon is in no way showing disrespect to the father of gods and men and to Hermes his offspring, in turning to salute his friend, the soldier Paralus three tiers above him, or in leaning to whisper informally to the companion at his side. "We are at Delphi, I presume."

Unquestionably the row of Doric pillars, set on a raised dais approached by four or five steps, before which the speaker of the prologue is standing, represents the famous temple of Phoebos.

Caierophon scarcely listens to the words. His mind still concerned with the same problem of city-revenue, catches a phrase, a name here and there, as one of us, tired and a little bored, might still untangle an already familiar *motif* or *leit-motif* from an obscure Tristram or Siegfried overture, and at the same time, recall matters of the day, a gown tried on or a tea-party or its masculine equivalent, so-and-so at the club or I must find a new tailor. We, as Caierophon, must bridge life, art gradually.

Then as Caierophon's ears become accustomed to this melodious rhythm, he bends once more to a whisper, "our Euripides has condescended to the rabble, this fairy-tale is hardly suitable to so great an audience; it veils no doubt, some jibe at our distinguished contemporaries."

So far we may enter into the sophisticated mind of this most sophisticated and polished gathering the world has ever known. Then like children, we must follow simply the simple story outlined by the god Hermes, lord of the caduceus and of the sandals, "gold, rare, imperishable."

For the god is telling us that Helios, his brother, loved, as was customary among the Olympians, a maiden. This girl was Kreousa, descendant of Erechtheus, the mythical founder of

Athens. She bore a child and in fear of her father, exposed it on the rocks. The god Helios, not quite ignoble, sends his brother Hermes to bring the baby, the basket he lies in, his clothes and little wrappings to the temple at Delphi. There the child lives as a young priest, with certain duties. Kreousa, his mother, marries Xouthos, a neighboring prince. They have no child. The queen and her husband make a pilgrimage to Delphi (a customary pilgrim-journey not unlike that undertaken in later times on various pretexts to Rome) to enquire of the God of prophecy as to their fortune. Kreousa is desperate, the old god-like race of Erechthonius ends with her death.

The voice of the actor rings clear now, whisperings have died away. The God, he explains, will give this very child to Xouthos, persuade him that it is his own; the boy shall enter his mother's palace, obtain his inheritance, yet keep secret the mystery of his birth.

We know in brief the story of the play, its beginning and its end.

Toward the back of the stage, half-hidden by the pillars, the young actor appears.

The speaker of the prologue turns: "but I see Helios' son approaches to sweep the porch with his laurel-branch." He steps toward the right. "I—and I first—call him by his own name— Ion."

II

THE BOY comes slowly down the steps. He wears a tunic, simply folded, embroidered with heavy work of gold thread. Perhaps as a young priest, he wore the tall boots, attribute of Helios, slayer of death and gloom in the Monster Python. From the words of the prologue just spoken we know that he carries a branch or small bundle of laurel-twigs.

At this moment if the Greek drama were grand-opera, the heavy, more or less ponderous and complex overture, the blending of many instruments, would evolve itself into one theme. If we were trained musicians we would have been aware of the alteration of mood about two-thirds through the speech of

Hermes. But as god disappears, the notes become light, easy to follow. The main instruments are strings, notably the harp or *phorminx*, adopted by the God, accompaniment to inspired speech and prophetic utterance.

The boy comes slowly forward and pauses. The two lines of young priests who have entered from opposite sides, join in a single half-circle at the back of the stage below the temple pillars.

Ion lifts his laurel branch.

Armata men tade lampra tethrippon.

Hail chariot and chariot-driver, God about to step toward us over the untrodden peaks, to step down the mountain-passes toward us, your lovers, your children.

His words, the sound, the subtly accented rhythm, above all the swift bright flow, the movement of the whole, acts upon us, bears the same relation to our nerves, our nervous organism, as music, but is as far above ordinary music, we might be tempted to say, as music is above common speech.

There is no adequate translation for the Greek words and there never will be.

The mere skeleton runs something like this:

Helios' chariot
four-abreast,
fagot-torch,
sets fire to earth;
out of the ether,
stars flee from this star
into the holy night;
Parnassus'
unconquered heights
catch light while the sun-disc
swims into mortal sight
with myrrh
above the roof,
smoke
from dried incense-branch,
while on the Delphic seat
the high priestess waits
to chart the God's will
unto the Greeks.

We see with the eyes of the young actor, not the row of priests and officials, not the circle above them; writer, statesman, sculptor, Caierophon and Apollodorus, the whole body of aristocratic Athens, the well-born, the spiritually well-endowed, nor yet the mass of bourgeois, the Gastrons and Drekons, crowding tier on tier above them. But with the eyes of a young priest and with the eyes of a poet we see Parnassus, the mountain that has stood for just a second before actual dawn, black against the silver-grey of the false-dawn, in just that second become two peaks, jagged, in exquisite outline, until every detail becomes suddenly visible, and through the twin-peaks there pours a fire, pours and swirls upward, and the whole sky above is mad with the riot, and the runnels and channels and dried ditches of the rocky mountain are filled with gold.

The music of the lines, as an accompaniment of strings following a song may continue with light variation after the actual song is finished, lingers, for a few beats, after the boy has finished speaking.

Ion turns. Almost with a sharp voice, almost with the tones of a *chausseur* urging forward the hounds, or that of the goal-keeper at the moment when the charioteers drop their tense posture of expectancy and the taut reins fall loose on the flanks of great steeds, almost his voice takes such a clear deep resonance as he turns to the row of youthful priests attending him.

> *Go,*
> *go Delphic priests,*
> *cleanse and purify your spirits*
> *in Kastalia's silver pool-depth;*
> *wholly purified, come back,*
> *speak as he would have you speak,*
> *word for word the mystic writ,*
> *soothsayers and holy prophets,*
> *unto those who seek*
> *his help.*

The boy pauses again, the priests have gone, the pattern, the frieze one might almost say against which he has been standing, is changed to another. The precise posture of the row of attending youths (even although we have been but half-conscious of their presence) has had the same effect upon our nerves, as a plaque in low-relief against which some fine statue of the *duodemonos* or young athlete might stand. But we become conscious of the fine vigour of this *basso-relievo* only when the boy turns, only when he himself notices it, leaving the single figure slight, intense and frail against the great, ribbed pillar of the temple-portico.

He continues in a lower voice, as if explaining half to himself, his position, his relative worth and his insignificance in face of the emblems of worship surrounding him.

This is my work:
even as a mere youth,
with chaplet of flowers
and laurel in the new leaf,
I made fragrant the steps
and the threshold of Helios:
I sprinkled the pavement,
showering water-drops:
and with my swift darts
frightened the bird-flocks,
that would perch on the temple-gifts.
I put them to sudden flight:
fatherless, motherless,
alone in the temple-gates,
I praise Helios,
my source of life.

Then as if the god himself had touched him, as he rings from his own *phorminx* his own most lovely music, the boy is caught, torn from his quiet worship. He has become enraptured, one with the God, merged into him, fire of song, spark of a greater fire. He is Hyacinth whom the god loved. We close our eyes to shut out sound and the vision of our fellow-beings dark beside us, inert and stagnant, in their circle of stone-benches. But most of all to escape this vision, the boy caught, struggling, a white bird in a great wind, a flower, exposed to the sun.

Come, laurel,
beloved, most sweet,

(O shoot, leaf and new-leaf
        and flower, beautiful to sweep
        beneath altar, across pavement)
from flower-slopes
where gods walk:
where crystal streams,
swift water-paths
feed the roots
of holy myrtle-plants,
with whose branch too I sweep
precinct
pavement;
all day,
day-long I work
from the first dawn-hint
of the fire-wings,
I greet
Paion,
O Paion,
king,
priest;
may you be for ever blest,
Latona's child,
loveliest.

Ah, but the task is sweet,
cleaning your threshold, Phoebos,
worshipping the mysteries:
ah, but his task is slight
who serves a god,
a deathless spirit,
never weariness can touch
a servant of such rapture servant,
Helios is father-spirit:
hail, Helios, my pledge of life,
father, father, through the house
I speak your name
intent to worship

Paion,
O Paion,

king,
priest;
may you be for ever blest,
Latona's child,
loveliest.

He pauses. The boy reaches toward the flask or jar of beaten gold, which stands on one of the upper steps, its shape, half-lost in the shadow beneath the pillar.

Ion lifts the jar, holds it in the curve of one arm. With stiff, precise movements (perfect in rhythm with the turn of the head) he scatters spray on spray of water into the open porch of the temple and across the steps below him.

Now I must finish this,
drop my laurel-branch,
take the pitcher,
this golden flask of water,
fresh as when the earth
sprayed it from Kastalia's rocks;
I, a spirit, unharassed,
scattering the sacred drops,
pray: Helios, may I never cease
this service but for gracious death.

What is this note of death? It seems from the bright exultation of the boy's voice to refer to some knowledge, to hint of some joy, guessed at or actually experienced in the mysteries of the inner worship to which he has perhaps gained admittance, sanctioned as foster-child and favourite of the priests and of the god.

But we have not time to speculate on this for the boy starts from his reverie, places his jar once more upon the step and with a sudden movement reaches for a tall bow standing against the pillar.

With a shout he bounds down the steps. Is some Python about to rear a black head from among the bays where Hermes has lately hid himself, or some barbarian, enemy to beauty, rush out from the bushes? But no, we gather from the movement of the head and the bending of the slender throat that it is something in the air above that has startled Ion.

Birds,
you dart from Parnassus,
then back to Parnassus;
you rest on the roof,
the roof-peak, the gold cornice;
ah legate of Zeus,
tyrant of small flocks:
this match for claw and beak
my arrow threatens—
swift, be off.

O swan,
O slow-drifting next,
O bird of the scarlet feet,
is no other place fair enough,
but this, but his holiest,
no marsh-land
no field of Delos?
Ah swift,
for the song-note,
tuned to the god's bright phorminx,
cannot heal, O bird,
a blood-stained throat.

What fluttering—
a new bird this,
and she, actually she rests,
with wisps of straw
beneath the cornice;
my bow repeats the threat,
be off, lest grass and twigs
should litter up
the offerings set about the porch;
my arrow warns you;
rather hatch your brood
along the river Alpheus,
or further yet,
in Isthmian thickets.
Be off—I must do my work,
my duty to the gods and priests.

> but birds, birds,
> how can I hurt
> you, messengers,
> God's voice on earth.

We seem to hear through the movement and power of the Greek words, the whirr of swift arrows, the fluttering of many wings. And we wonder what birds these are that the boy sees in his imagination; this "new bird" that he speaks of, was it some rare crane or ibis flying from Egypt across the desert and the Corinthian-gulf, that had once startled the poet with blue-black gleam of its velvet throat and its spotted wings, as he visited Delphi, and as a child perhaps, escaped from the temple to follow the flare of colour against the mountain, to watch the flight of some flamingo-like bird, fire against the pinnacle of fire?

III

THE BOY rests on an upper step beneath one of the great side-pillars and we lose sight of him momentarily, as a group of women enter from the opposite side.

These ladies are not inmates of the temple. We judge from the elaborate blending of gold and silver ornaments, the fine braiding of hair, the well-chosen and costly garments, that they are women of some worldly standing. From the first words of the speaker we learn that they are Athenians.

> Not in Athens where the gods walk,
> are the porches set about,
> pillar by pillar
> with more beautiful work,
> nor shrines before the highways
> for their worship:
> but here, too at the seat
> of the God-prophet, Latona begot,
> light strikes beauty
> from twin-wrought temple-fronts.

They are astonished at the beauty of the temple. They separate, two by two, or one wanders alone to examine closely the paintings beyond the pillars, set, we are led to believe, in the inner-porch. We cannot see these pictures but from the informal conversation of these women, we can almost reconstruct line from line the paintings, perhaps imagined of the poet (himself a painter in youth) or else graphically described from sketches seen in the atelier of some friend or from the finished work intended to stand on the Acropolis (as yet unrecovered from the attack of the Persians) still in the hands of architect and sculptor.

> *Here, see the son of Zeus,*
> *look—my friend—bend close—*
> *threatens with a golden knife*
> *the snake of the Lernian marsh.*

These stately women become eager, excited—"see—see," drawing attention to this, to that detail as they recall early friezes perhaps remembered as children in some small rustic temple in the environs of Athens, or some detail of a god's life they stitched as young girls in Athens' temple-porches.

> *Yes, yes, and near it,*
> *another lifts a bright torch,*
> *who is it—I have wrought*
> *his deeds across my distaff—*
> *ah, he who took the god's hurt*
> *sharing his dire grief,*
> *the spearsman, Iolaus.*

> *Ah this—but see this,*
> *a youth on a winged horse,*
> *is slaying a monstrous beast*
> *three-bodied with fiery breath.*

> *We gaze about—see—*
> *across the walls of rock,*
> *the rout of the earth-born giants.*

So they pass from picture to picture. And I should be inclined to believe that the poet had in mind some series, highly decorative, in low relief—rather than paintings—for we notice he has not once employed that so marvellous word *kuaneas*, the

Greek blue, nor any hint of saffron nor purple-black shadows such as Pindar, for example, uses in his famous passage, descriptive of the birth of this very Ion. But there is everywhere gold. We follow the gesture of the Athenian woman, surprising in each inset, some glitter of gold-leaf or ornament of dark gold. From the metallic gleam of Heracles' scimitar, our eyes trace the intricate, decorative twisting of the dragon and with the slash of its tail are led upward to gold again, the torch held aloft by the young hero, Iolaus. Perhaps dripping of gold sparks leads our eyes down again to wonder at the head of the next beast, "fire-breathing": once more the fire is gold.

We note this—

She shakes an aegis,
dragon-wrought,
threatening Enkeladous.

Ah, Pallas, my goddess!
Fire this and fire-bolt,
in the far-reaching hands of Zeus.

So from the gold or brass, gleaming, we may imagine, from the barbaric bracelets on the fore-arms of the giants, we are drawn from a raised fore-arm to the circle of the great shield which the mighty Titaness brandishes, Athené, the goddess.

The shield-rim is set in gold and there is gold again in the lightning-spears of Zeus and a gold head-band, we might imagine, about the head of the peaceful Dionysus. They pause together before the last picture.

With his fire-shaft he strikes,
shattering the giant, Mimos,
and Bromios, the glad heart,
with ivy-staff (not meant for this)
slays another child of earth.

They turning, they find the boy Ion seated on the steps.

IV

He has risen now and stands.

He, as servant of the temple is accustomed to the sight of strangers, the drift of pilgrims of all classes and all countries. And he regards the leader of the band as she steps forward, calmly without special interest.

She asks him if they may enter the temple.

"No," he says and adds, "it is not customary."

"May we converse then, with you, one of the temple servants?"

"That, yes—what is it?"

"Is it true that Helios' temple really does rest on the very heart of the earth?"

He answers "indeed yes"—fragrant with garlands—offerings of scented flowers, laurels and azaleas and great mass and spike of flowers from mountain-bush and tree—and he adds "dragons watch it."

"Such was the common tale," the Athenian lady answers, anxious now that the boy should realise them as not quite ignorant of the temple and temple-myth.

He sees now that these are no ordinary sight-seers and he unbends a little, telling them of the custom of sacrificing before entering the temple, bloodless sacrifice, the archaic wheat, honey and oil-cake, but after, real blood-sacrifice is required if they intend to visit the inner-shrine.

The woman thanks him, saying they will transgress no sacred custom, but wait outside and examine further the beautiful detail of the porches.

"Do so, by all means," and the woman answers that their mistress has always wanted them to see this.

"Of what house are you called servants?"

> Our mistress is of Athens;
> the porches of Pallas are her court—
> you ask of her—she is present.

V

SHE HAS ENTERED unnoticed this tall woman, Kreousa, child of Erechtheus, queen of Athens. And she stands, motionless, a statue almost wrought of lapis, we might think, so intense a blue is her robe, falling in straight folds to her feet.

The boy moves toward her, but she does not speak.

The attendant-women scatter silently through the porches and disappear.

Again the boy moves, wondering at the strange, intense beauty of this face. And still she does not speak or turn, her eyes on the temple-porch.

"O noble, of most noble birth" the boy begins, he, the child and fosterling of the temple, nameless, humble before this presence, falters, waits and then:

O noble of birth,
beautiful in appearance,
you have that look,
whoever you are, O woman,
that most men, seeing your face
would know
you were sprung of a great people;
but what is this—
it comes as a shock to me,
those half-shut eyes, staining with tears
that proud face,
even after you have looked
at the altar of Helios.

Oh lady,
with what thought do you approach,
for most, seeing the god's house,
laugh out—only you
weep at the sight.

She turns, the rapt face softens, the statue's face changed into a woman's as she becomes conscious of this other, its youth and austere charm. As if speaking aloud her thoughts, she answers, impelled by some unquestionable power, some strange rapport between them.

> *Fair lad,*
> *it is not unplaced*
> *that you wonder seeing me weep,*
> *but as I look upon this, Helios' house,*
> *old memory stabs afresh,*
> *and though standing here,*
> *I am, as it were, alone*
> *in my own place,*
> *and I think:*
> *how wretched, how miserable we women are,*
> *what sport for fate—yet what of this?*
> *how can we expect man's justice,*
> *we who perish by gods' injustice*
> *and their hate.*

He, accustomed to tales of sorrow, confidence of pilgrim and invalid seeking consolation in the famous shrine of healing, easily enters into her mood and would soften her bitterness.

He draws near and inquires simply: "why are you hurt, tortured and sad?"

As I had intended to outline only the opening chorus of the *Ion*, I should have concluded with the last words of the waiting women before the entrance of the queen. For the whole character of the play alters after her coming. The boy's faith is shadowed. We are plunged into political discussions, religious doubts and curious rather crude plot and counter-plot.

But it was hard to turn away. The queen was standing there a moment ago, in her blue garments. All of his queens are beautiful and there are others of Euripides' women that are robed in blue. Thetis especially I see, as she appears in the last scene of the *Andromeda*. But her robe is another blue, a gentian or hyacinth-blue, an unworldly, unearthly colour. But Kreousa, queen of Athens, wears the blue of stones, lapis-blue, the blue of the fire in the earth, a blue that seems to symbolize not only her pride and her power but also her passion and her loss.

NOTES ON EURIPIDES (EXCERPTS)

. . . some of Euripides' most exquisite love-lyrics perished with his great Love drama. . . . Those lyrics were stained with ineffable purity we do know and we may be sure with underlying psycho-physical intensity.

Such a play might even have risen to the spiritual-emotional heights of the Ionians. . . .

Is it not possible that the later censure that precluded so many of the most exquisite stanzas of Sappho, in like manner forbade these [love lyrics]? . . . Many of Euripides' surviving plays hold outright anti-war and anti-social protest. But erotic-emotional innovation is comparatively rare. An interesting point rises, is his real personal philosophy lost, what did these plays contain, how did they approach life? Surely, in some ultra-modern spirit if the surviving plays are any clue to the lost ones. Euripides was unpopular during his life as a free-thinker, and an iconoclast. It is save to assume that the lost plays held pertinent modern matter.

. . . Euripides lived through almost a modern great-war period. . . . How would 1917 London have acclaimed such anti-war propaganda? Work that out and you will have some idea of the power and detachment of the Attic dramatist. For we are too apt to pigeon-hole the Attic poets and dramatists, put them B.C. this or that, forget them in our survey of modern life and literature, not realizing that the whole spring of all literature (even of all life) is that one small plane-leaf of an almost-island, that tiny rock among the countries of a world, Hellas.

Look at the map of Greece. Then go away and come back and look and look and look at it. The jagged contours stir and inflame the imagination, time-riddled banner of freedom and fiery independence, a rag of a country, all irregular, with little torn-off bits, petals drifting, those islands, "lily on lily that o'er lace the sea." Look at the map of Greece. It is a hieroglyph. You will be unable to read it and go away and come back after years and just begin to spell out the meaning of its outline. Then you will realize that you know nothing at all about it and begin all over, learning a cryptic language. I am never tired of speculating on the power of that outline, just the mysterious line of it, apart from the thing it stands for. That leaf hanging a pendant to the whole of Europe seems to indicate the living strength and sap of the thing it derives from. Greece is indeed the tree-of-life, the ever-present stream, the spring of living water. . . .

. . . the lines of this Greek poet (and all Greek poets if we have but the clue) are today as vivid and as fresh as they ever were, but vivid and fresh not as literature (though they are that too) but as portals, as windows, as portholes I am tempted to say that look out from our ship our world, our restricted lives, on to a sea that moves and changes and bears us up, and is friendly and vicious in turn. These words are to me portals, gates.

I know that we need scholars to decipher and interpret the Greek, but we also need: poets and mystics and children to re-discover this Hellenic world, to see *through* the words; the word being but the outline, the architectural structure of that door or window, through which we are all free, scholar and unlettered alike, to pass. We emerge from our restricted minds (with all due reverence to them, of course) into a free, large, clear, vibrant, limitless realm, sky and sea and distant islands, and a shore-line such as this in Egypt and another along the coast of Asia Minor or further toward the Bosphorus, and again Greece, Hellas, the thousand intimate bays, the foaming straits.

Guy Davenport
7 Greeks

Here is a colorful variety of works by seven Greek poets and philosophers who lived from the eighth to the third centuries B.C. Salvaged from shattered pottery vases and tattered scrolls of papyrus, everything decipherable from the remains of these ancient poets is assembled here. From early to late, the collection contains: Archilochos; Sappho; Alkman; Anakreon; the philosophers Herakleitos and Diogenes; and Herondas. This composite of fragments translated by Guy Davenport is the most complete collection of its kind ever to appear in one volume.

"Overall, this volume will afford great pleasure to scholars, teachers and also those who simply love to watch delightful souls disport themselves in language."

—Anne Carson

Sam Hamill
The Infinite Moment

Drawing from the classic *Lyra Graeca* and *The Greek Anthology*, Sam Hamill has made new, American translations of poems in the thousand-year tradition that begins with Sappho, Alcaeus, and Anakreon in the 6th century B.C. and ends with Paulos Silentarios in the 6th century A.D. The love poems, epigrams, and sly invective of over forty poets remind us once again of the deep wellspring of ancient Greece that nourished the roots of so many cultures.

"Hamill's aim is to write poems that aim, as Greek poems usually did aim, not at readers but at listeners."
—William Arrowsmith

Ezra Pound
and Rudd Fleming
Sophokles' Elektra

Early in 1949, while under indictment for treason and hospital-
ized by court order at St. Elizabeths Hospital in Washington D.C.,
Ezra Pound collaborated with Rudd Fleming, a professor at the
University of Maryland, on a new version of Sophokles' *Elektra*.
Pound's decision to focus on this play of imprisonment and justice at such a crucial juncture in his own life and art throws both
the play and the poet into stark and ironic relief.

"For all the blankness of its language, the power and force of this
new look may give you an insight into what made Elektra tick—
like a time bomb."

—Clive Barnes, *The New York Post*

Ezra Pound
Sophokles' Women of Trachis

For Ezra Pound, Sophokles' *Women of Trachis* represented "the highest peak of Greek sensibility registered in any of the plays that have come down to us." Nothing rhetorical, nothing long-winded survives in Pound's version of Sophokles' tragedy. The language is lit with lights long extinguished in the traditionally ornate and airless verse translations. With no mincing, poetry speeds tragedy down its course to disaster.

"Pound's handling of the verses, especially the choruses, seems to me to be masterly. His ear is as faultless as ever."

—T. S. Eliot